ADLER

FOR BEGINNERS

by Anne Hooper and Jeremy Holford
Illustrated by Kathryn Hyatt

Writers and Readers Publishing, Inc.
P.O. Box 461, Village Station
New York, NY 10014

Writers and Readers Limited
35 Britannia Row
London N1 8QH
Tel: 0171 226 3377
Fax: 0171 359 1454
e-mail: begin@writersandreaders.com

A Writers and Readers Documentary Comic Book
Copyright © 1998
ISBN # 0-86316-270-3 Trade
1 2 3 4 5 6 7 8 9 0

Printed in Finland by WSOY

Beginners Documentary Comic Books are published by Writers and Readers Publishing, Inc. Its trademark, consisting of the words "For Beginners, Writers and Readers Documentary Comic Books," and the Writers and Readers logo, is registered in the U.S. Patent and Trademark Office and in other countries.

publishing FOR BEGINNERS™ books continuously since 1975:

1975: Cuba • 1976: Marx • 1977: Lenin • 1978: Nuclear Power • 1979: Einstein • Freud • 1980: Mao • Trotsky • 1981: Capitalism • 1982: Darwin • Economists • French REvolution • Marx's Kapital • Food • Ecology • 1983: DNA • Ireland • 1984: London • Peace • Medicine • Orwell • Reagan • Nicaragua • Black History • 1985: Mark Diary • 1986: Zen • Psychiatry • Reich • Socialism • Computers • Brecht • Elvis • 1988: Architecture • Sex • JFK • Virginia Woolf • 1990: Nietzsche • Plato • Malcolm X • Judaism • 1991: WWII • Erotica • African History • 1992: Philosophy • Rainforests • Miles Davis • Islam • Pan Africanism • 1993: Black Women • Arabs and Israel • 1994: Babies • Foucault • Heidegger • Hemingway • Classical Music • 1995: Jazz • Jewish Holocaust • Health Care • Domestic Violence • Sartre • United Nations • Black Holocaust • Black Panthers • Martial Arts • History of Clowns • 1996: Opera • Biology • Saussure • UNICEF • Kierkegaard • Addiction & Recovery • I Ching • Buddha • Derrida • Chomsky • McLuhan • Jung • 1997: Lacan • Shakespeare • Structuralism • Che • 1998: Fanon • Adler • Ghandi • Toni Morrison

ADLER
FOR BEGINNERS

Contents

THE BIG INTRODUCTION   6
Theory: Life-style   11

A FAMILY CONSTELLATION   13
Theory: Family Constellation   13

EARLY DAYS   15

EARLY RECOLLECTIONS   20
Theories: Early Recollections   20
        Private Logic   26

EDUCATION AND PERSONAL GROWTH   27
Theories: Adler's Educational Theories   30
        Movement and Consciousness   32
Biography: Carl Furtmuller   36

THE ONE BIG LOVE   38
Theories: Life Tasks   41
        Adler's Early Ideas on Child Rearing   44

THE START OF A BRILLIANT CAREER   46
Theories: Adlerian Counselling Methods   48
        The Impact of the Outside World on Personal Development   49

ADLER AND FREUD: EARLY DAYS   51
Biography: Sigmund Freud   51

GAINING FREUD'S ESTEEM   56
Theory: Foundations fo the Theory of the Inferiority Complex   58

ORGAN INFERIORITY   60
Theory: The Drive to Feel Equal   61

THE GREAT DISPUTE   64
Theories: The Agression Drive   65
        The Inferiority Complex coupled with Masculine Protest   69

DIRTY WORK AT THE CROSSROADS: THE SPLIT WITH FREUD   72
Theory: Sex   75

A GROUP OF ONE'S OWN   77

THE NEUROTIC CONSTITUTION   80
Biographies: Nietzsche   80
        Hans Vaihinger   81

Theories: The Law of Ideational Shifts   82
         Acting "As If"   83
         Guiding Fictions   83
         The Development of Neuroses   84

THE BIRTH OF INDIVIDUAL PSYCHOLOGY   86

A TIME OF HORRORS: THE GREAT WAR   88
Theories: Gemeinshaftsgefuhl (Social Interest)   91
         Cooperation   93
         Birth Order   95

MARITAL CHANGE   96
Theory: Marriage   97

NEW VIENNA AND THE NEW ADLERIAN MOVEMENT   100
Theories: Encouragement   101
         Taking Responsibility   102
         The Goals of Children   104
Biography: Walter Beran Wolfe   110

PREPARING FOR THE PILGRIMAGE TO THE NEW WORLD   111
Theories: Priorities   112
         Dreams   116

ADLER DISCOVERS THE NEW WORLD   117

ADLER - THE STAR   123

TALES OF THE VIENNA WOULDS   126

THE RISE OF THE NAZIS   128
Theory: Personality Types   133

THE FINAL YEARS   134

BEYOND THE GRAVE   141
Theories: Four Principles of Conflict Resolution   143
         Paradoxical Intent   145
         Change   148

ADLER IN THE 21st CENTURY   150

LAST WORDS   151

APPENDIX   152
Address of Adlerian Institutes and Associations in USA, Canada,
United Kingdom, Eire, plus International Associations and Summer Schools

ADDITIONAL READING   154

The Big Introduction

We'd like to introduce Adler, **ALFRED ADLER**, founding father of Individual Psychology, educationalist, best-selling author and practical philosopher.

You've heard about **Freud**.
You've heard about **Jung**.

Now meet
ADLER...
the man who gave us

- The INFERIORITY COMPLEX
- Power trips
- Control freaks
- Life Tasks
- Life-style
- Goal-oriented behaviour
- Social interest

(and much, much more).

Yes, the one and only **ALFRED ADLER** (1870 - 1937).

Who influenced folks like:

Victor Frankl
Carl Rogers
Abraham Maslow

and ideas like:

logotherapy
cognitive therapy
neuro-linguistic programming

Adler's life was packed with contrasts.

He trained as a physician, became a psychologist and educationalist, pro-feminist and skilled public speaker. Adler was a friend of Trotsky's but received support and backing from American millionaires.

Adler believed in personal freedom, social responsibility and the rights of children and women.

The Danish sculptor Tyra Boldsen planned a monument showing 99 famous women and one man:

ALFRED ADLER.

He was so famous that the Gershwins wrote a song about him (and Freud and Jung) for their musical *"Pardon My English."*

So let's look at some of Adler's basic ideas. He saw people as **creative, self-determining individuals with a subjective outlook**, i.e. the world is not how others see it, but how WE see it. He took a holistic view of people: the **complete** person is what counts, not just some parts like the sex drive. Adlerian analysis is respectful; ideas about a person's behaviour and motives are **suggestions**, not statements. The individual is the expert on their personality and may just need guidance to understand what makes them tick.

Human behaviour is goal-oriented and all behaviour is socially-embedded - nobody exists right outside society. We are born into social groups called families. You can turn your back on society, but remember: even the loneliest hermit had a ma and pa.

A lot of our behaviour has the goal of moving us from a feeling of minus to a feeling of plus, from inferiority to superiority. Those people who always feel inferior, are really suffering from faulty thinking. More about inferiority and SUPERIORITY later on.

TO MOVE FROM MINUS TO PLUS, THERE ARE THREE IMPORTANT AREAS IN LIFE YOU HAVE TO GET RIGHT:

Work
Friendship
and shucks, gosh, **Intimacy.**

Adler called these the **Life Tasks**; your beliefs about the Tasks and approach to them decide what kind of personality you develop.

Adler called the individual's whole personality the **Life-style**; Life-style is also a set of ideas, of convictions, each of us has about ourselves, the others and the world. Our behaviour is consistent with those ideas. The process of uncovering such concepts is called **Life-style Analysis**.

Theory: LIFE STYLE

How a child learns to become established within the family (so there is a feeling of belonging) helps develop its Life-style, literally its style of dealing with life. This style is formed partly by seeing how other family members react to different behaviours and attitudes and partly from conclusions the child draws within itself. An individual's Life-style is his/her way of 'acting, thinking and perceiving' and a 'scheme for ways to live'. From this Life-style we select methods of coping with the Life Tasks. Where Adler differs from psycho-analytical thought is that he makes no separation between conscious and unconscious, Instead he believed that humans choose their behaviour, rather than are driven by unconscious urges. Men and women see their lives in certain ways because these perceptions suit their Life-styles.

Life-style is formed early on, between the ages of four and six. Getting people to talk about their **early recollections** (ERs to Adlerians) is an effective way of beginning Life-style Analysis. And Early Recollections happen from the day you were born and have to fit yourself into...

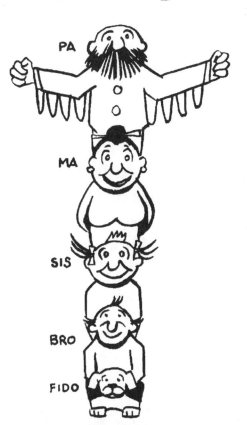

PA

MA

SIS

BRO

FIDO

The family constellation locates the members by birth order and reveals groupings of children. But as well as the physical birth order, the constellation can be used in Life-style Analysis to show the psychological birth order in the family.

Theory: FAMILY CONSTELLATION

How we see the grouping of family members, (the particular ties or emotional bonds, varying ages, the dominance or submission of particular family members) will affect how we develop. Adler believes that interaction between family members is the most **significant** element in firming the child's personality. Each child is born into a unique position in the family which he/she sees subjectively. This means the child forms a unique perspective of the world, regardless of sharing the same home.

For instance, eldest children can feel dethroned by the arrival of younger siblings and seek extra attention through bad behaviour. But they can also take on a caring role for the little 'uns, acting like an extra parent. Eldests are often high achievers, perfectionists, superior and exactly what a second child wants to rebel against. (Adler was a second child and often rowed with big brother Sigmund.)

Now, suppose the eldest child is sick or has some kind of disability, the second child may take on the role of eldest and be the boss, the carer, the one who gets things done. So, you see, the place in the psychological order can be changed. Being an eldest son or an eldest daughter in a family where there are same sex siblings also has meaning, as does the previous existence of siblings who may have died, even in utero.

Your place in the constellation matters because it can affect you, throughout life.

WAIT A MINUTE, WAIT A MINUTE.

THAT'S ENOUGH OF THE BIG INTRODUCTION.

LISTEN, YOU TELL THE STORY OF MY LIFE AND WORK.

I CAN BUTT IN AND COMMENT WHEN I WANT TO. RIGHT?

RIGHT. TO BEGIN AT THE BEGINNING.

Early Days

Alfred Adler was born on Monday,
February 7th, 1870, at
Rudolfsheim near Vienna.
His parents, Leopold and
Pauline had married in
1866; their first child,
Sigmund, was
born in 1868.
Five more
children
arrived
by 1884.

He was socially confident:

It's no surprise that Adler's theories stressed the social value of fitting in. One of his main ideas is **Gemeinschaftsgefuhl**, usually translated as **Social Interest**.

Okay. Even though he liked people, Alfred was never very close to his parents. He spent a lot of time with his younger brothers and sisters when they were kids, but Alfred was not when they grew up.

Remember what we told you about the eldest child being dethroned by the second? Guess what happened... That's right: big brother Sigmund and Alfred fought and struggled to get noticed by their parents. Sigmund thought he was boss, but Alfred was always too much of an individual to agree.

(A few years later another bossy Sigmund would try to shove Adler into line.)

SIGI und ALFI

17

Most of the time, the Adlers were a big, happy bunch.

Leopold and Pauline weren't great readers but they loved music. Alfred was a talented singer. Leopold and Pauline once came home to find their three-year-old standing on the piano singing a dirty song.

Leopold concluded that his son had been taken by the nursemaid to a low-life cabaret. He fired her. Alfred wasn't too sad: no nursemaid meant no rules and more chances for fun and games.

Adler always enjoyed life but as he grew older he acquired a lot of self-discipline. Perhaps he learnt something about control from his father's rigid thinking on moral subjects.

Papa Leopold always:

- **rose at 5am.**
- **had a walk before breakfast**
- **went to bed at 7pm. winter and summer.**

Such unbreakable routine was not so unusual in men of that generation but Leopold's refusal to move to one side of the staircase should he meet someone coming up, does raise a few questions about Leopold's own controlling behaviour! How would such inflexibility rebound on the sensitive lad?

Yet in contrast to these idiosyncrasies is the story of how Leopold corrected Alfred's greediness. Apparently the boy always snatched the largest helping at mealtimes. Leopold dealt with this quietly one day by setting before him the entire dish of dumplings, telling him "We will eat what you leave". Did this give the young gourmand an early lesson about learning from the results of his own actions? This is possibly, a clear example of Adler's own later technique for handling young children.

Early Recollections

Your Life-style (essential personality) is developed by the time you are six or seven years old. Adlerians start to analyse the Life-style by asking clients for memories - or Earliest Recollections (ERs) - of those years.

Theory: EARLY RECOLLECTIONS

A client's Early Recollections are used by therapists to gain insight into a person's Life-style. They are the memories of specific incidents in childhood, from birth up till about six or seven years of age. These memories *"are, for the client, his 'story of my life,' a story he repeats to himself to warn him or comfort him, by means of past experiences, to meet the future with an already tested plan of action."* — Adler

In Life-style analysis, the client is asked

1. **To remember an incident in detail.**
2. **What is the most vivid moment of the memory?**
3. **What are the emotions evoked?**
4. **What is it that made you feel…these emotions?**

One method that condenses this technique is after remembering, to freeze the incident in memory as a "snapshot" and to give the "snapshot" a title. These earliest memories are important because they reveal beliefs, mistaken ideas which may have formed the basis for the way in which the client subsequently shaped his/her life. They also explain presently held attitudes, outlooks and motives.

Alfred himself had some pretty dramatic Early Recollections. Here are two.

1 **He recalled being about two years old and wrapped in bandages because of rickets. Big brother Sigmund moved about effortlessly; Alfred had to struggle to move at all.**

We might read from this that Alfred felt in later life he had to struggle to do things that his brother did effortlessly. Part of Alfred's Life-style could have been that life was a struggle and he must therefore devise exceptional strategies to cope.

2 When he was four, his small brother Rudolf caught diphtheria. Doctors knew little about the disease, apart from the fact that it was often fatal. Nobody suggested moving Alfred out of the room he shared with Rudolf.

"I woke up one morning. Rudolf lay alongside me. Dead."

This ER might have meant that the message young Alfred received was that small boys were extremely vulnerable and needed help which they didn't always get. He may have felt both helpless and rebellious in turn. It might even have been the foundation for his desire to become medically qualified.

The funeral gave him a further traumatic ER. When somebody comforted his mother, she smiled. Alfred was horrified: a mother smiling, at her son's funeral? For a long time Alfred could not forget or forgive that tiny smile. His Life-style consequence might have been a belief that mothers were happy when their children died.

Alfred was five when a bout of pneumonia nearly killed him. He remembered hearing the physician say there wasn't any point in looking after the boy: he was going to die. Alfred was so scared of dying he made a rapid recovery.

"I decided right then I would become a doctor and find weapons to fight death. And be a better doctor than the one who treated me."

Not everyone can remember - or wants to recall - their childhood experiences. So what happens to them? Adlerian analysts ask people to invent ERs because the kind of stories they create are **just as revealing** as true events.

Young Adler's personal experience proved it. This kid who wanted to conquer death had to walk past a cemetery on the way to school every day. It was spooky and he was scared. He saw other kids crossing the graveyard and was angry with himself for not being as brave.

"I decided to stop being scared. One day I let the other kids go ahead, then I ran through the cemetery and back, and through it and back until the fear vanished."

As an adult, he went to see this important site. And found the cemetery did not exist. It was just a necessary image for his Life-style.

The other founders of modern psychology had some interesting Early Recollections. Freud remembered wetting the bed and promising his father he'd buy a new one.

Carl Gustav Jung had an ER of visiting a museum with an aunt. He wanted to stop and look at the nude statues. The aunt hauled him out of the gallery yelling "Disgusting child, cover your eyes!"

Finding a place within the family and creating beliefs constructs the personal idea of how life works. However, because a child sees only with childish eyes, and employs a childish logic, the conclusions reached often result in mistaken ideas. These are what Adlerians call **Private**.

Theory: PRIVATE LOGIC

Adlerians believe that you are what you think. Life-style is built upon deeply established personal constructs, the individual's private logic. As we grow older we establish ideas about what is right or wrong about life, taken from purely subjective personal experience. If our early experiences have proved painful, this logic may be built on what others would term 'mistaken ideas'. For example, if a child does not feel significant to the family in a useful fashion, he or she will find a way to fit in, that is negative and useless. This private logic might include the thought that the best way to gain attention is by having a tantrum.

A further example would be that of a hypochondriac - someone who, through their imaginary illnesses, is constantly seeking reassuring attention. In early life this person may have learned that as far as attention goes illness is a winner. Their private logic therefore becomes, "when I am ill my needs are met". However the downside is that when they need real emotional reassurance they don't know how to ask for it or get it. By now, people imagine they are probably crying wolf.

The Theory So Far

- We are all self-creating beings
- We have a subjective view of the world
- All behaviour is goal-directed
- All behaviour is socially-embedded
- We are born into a human group and have to find our place in a Family Constellation
- Each person's Life-style (literally its style of dealing with life) is created in the first few years of life
- Early Recollections are a key to finding out about Life-style
- Private logic is composed of ideas conceived in infancy which may or may not be appropriate to later life

Education and Personal Growth

In 1979 Alfred arrived as a new boy at a school called the Communales Real-Und Obergymnasium. To save breath everybody used the nickname "Sperlaum," because it was in the Sperlgasse district.

(Now guess who had been a pupil there 14 years before? Herr S. Freud.)

Little Alfred was a year too young to enrol so Leopold and Pauline had done some fancy work on the truth. Alfred was not happy at the Sperlaum. The other boys were very competitive, the teaching was rigid and monotonous. All the students had to study:

- **Latin**
- **Greek**
- **history**
- **geography**
- **physics**
- **mathematics**
- **religion**

plus German literature, history and language.

Maths was the worst class for Adler. He failed the first year exams and had to repeat the whole year. His father was so angry he threatened to send him to work for a shoemaker.

Alfred switched schools in 1881 to the Heralsergymnasium. He felt happier there and stayed until he was 18. Even mathematics stopped being a problem after he solved a calculation that the teacher had failed to complete.

"... I liked math. I got to be one of the best in the school at it. This made me see that ideas about being born with special gifts and talents were wrong."

The teachers said little about their pupil's triumph. Education was concerned with pointing out mistakes, not about encouraging effort and praising success. Rules were strict and always enforced. Even the older pupils had to put up their hands to get permission to go to the lavatory.

When Adler developed his educational theories, they were radically different from those of his professors.

Theory: ADLER'S EDUCATIONAL THEORIES

1. Children are not born good or evil, but can be 'influenced' in either direction.

2. If children consistently mis-behave, it means there is logic (somewhere) beneath their actions. In other words, children's behaviour is purposeful just like adults - everything they do has a goal.

3. Adler stressed the use of natural and logical consequences when training children. He believed that the best way forward for the child is to discover what works and what doesn't work for them-selves - by learning from experience. There is no punishment/reward system.

4. Parents must be consistent with their own behaviour.

5. Encouragement is extremely valuable.

Alfred's teens and school years were mostly happy, but he was still jealous of his elder brother and stayed that way until he reached middle-age.

In 1889, when Alfred was 13, the family moved to the countryside just outside Vienna. Adler loved the open air; the sickly boy turned into an active young man. He wasn't tall but he was strong and enjoyed hiking and mountain climbing.

Theory: MOVEMENT AND CONSCIOUSNESS

Movement and consciousness went together in Adler's view. If you want to make progress, you need consciousness to plan your movements, watch for danger and give purpose to your actions. He believed that people move both psychologically and physically. Humans are constantly in motion, moving towards goals, which are private to the individual and are often unconscious. The pace, direction and manner of psychological and bodily movement tend to form a personal pattern; observing that pattern can make it possible to predict somebody's future actions. However some movements are common to all people in a society, like covering the mouth when lying. They make up the 'body language' which others can read.

Adler learnt to move with great elegance and poise. In his sixties he taught a friend how to walk on sheet ice without slipping over.

In Spring, 1888, Adler graduated from the 'Hernals' gymnasium with a career in medicine mapped out. He wanted to be a hands-on doctor, actively helping people, rather than researching in some gloomy laboratory.

Alfred arrived at the University of Vienna Medical School for pre-med training in the Fall of 1888. He was starting a seven year course that stressed diagnosis and experimentation but contained nothing about how a physician could soothe a patient's fears or deal with other than their medical needs.

The Vienna professors were not forward-looking or open to new ideas. In 1847, the obstetrician Semmelweiss discovered that childbed fever was caused by doctors going from the operating theatre straight to the birth scene without washing their hands. This theory upset the medical profession. Semmelweiss was insulted and mocked right up to the day of his death in 1861.

Adler signed up only for those courses he had to take to become qualified. Psychiatry was not obligatory, so Alfred missed Herr Instructor Freud lecturing on hysteria. He did show up at Kraft-Ebing's course on diseases of the nervous system and read Kraft-Ebing's famous book on sexual deviation.

One part of his studies Adler always remembered with pleasure was taught by Hermann Nothnagel. Like Adler, Nothnagel became a doctor in order to help people. He believed in treating patients with care and courtesy and his favourite saying was **"Only a good man can be a great physician."**

There was time to relax after lectures and Alfred made full use of it. His favourite past-time was meeting friends at the Cafe Griensteidl to talk philosophy, politics, medicine and plain old-fashioned gossip. The taste for company stayed with Adler all his life; he was happiest in groups.

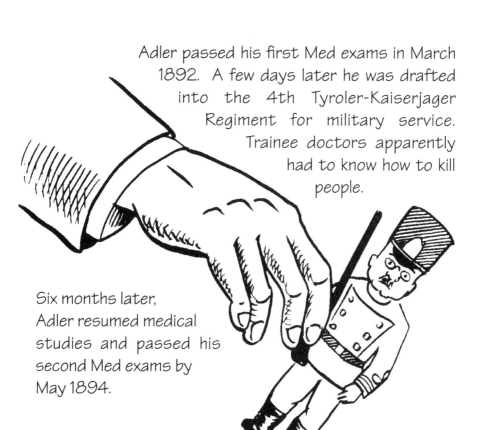

Adler passed his first Med exams in March 1892. A few days later he was drafted into the 4th Tyroler-Kaiserjager Regiment for military service. Trainee doctors apparently had to know how to kill people.

Six months later, Adler resumed medical studies and passed his second Med exams by May 1894.

To get experience, medical students had to work at the General Hospital or the Poliklinik, a free medical centre for the poor. Catch: only Austrians could work at the General Hospital and Adler was technically a Hungarian—he took Austrian nationality only in 1911. So it was the Poliklinik for him.

On 22nd November 1895, Adler made his parents proud: they could talk about "our son, the doctor". His medical degree was awarded.

Dr Adler continued working at the Poliklinik until the army claimed him for the second dose of military life. Posted to a Hungarian regiment, he was registered as 'Aladar Adler' and served in a military hospital.

As a medical student, like many others before him, Alfred became politicised. The path he veered towards was socialism. The alternative was nationalism which was not really a viable choice for someone of

Jewish origin. His socialist interests nudged Adler towards intellectual Marxist circles where he tended to be a listener rather than a speaker. Marx's economic theories bored Adler and he never fully understood them.

But Marx's ideas did turn Adler's attention to society: to the way people find ways to fit into it and to the effect society can have on individuals. These new ideas found fertile ground in the shape of feelings already established in his childhood, such as the camaraderie he had experienced with friends. The Marxist explanation of how the established social situation influences the individual's intellectual and emotional life helped form the basis of his own philosophy.

As an idealistic student, he began to put into clearer form concepts that he had always held during childhood about the value of friendship regardless of class.

Once qualified, the bright and brisk Dr. Adler worked hard and continued to take his pleasure as he had done as a student, meeting friends in coffee houses. At the Cafe Dom he encountered young men with more practical interests in politics. One of them was **Carl Furtmuller** who became a life-long friend and co-worker.

BIOGRAPHY

CARL FURTMULLER

The educator CARL FURTMULLER was a life-long friend and colleague of Adler.

At the age of 21 he was elected as the youngest member of the founding board of the Volksheim, Austria's first center for adult education at which Adler himself would later lecture. He supported Adler through all his moves, editing the first edition of the journal for Individual Psychology. After the First World War he was a founder of the movement in Vienna to train teachers in Adlerian child cguidance methods. In those early years when the two men were students his views on the importance of educational reform as a vital foundation for social change strongly affected Adler.

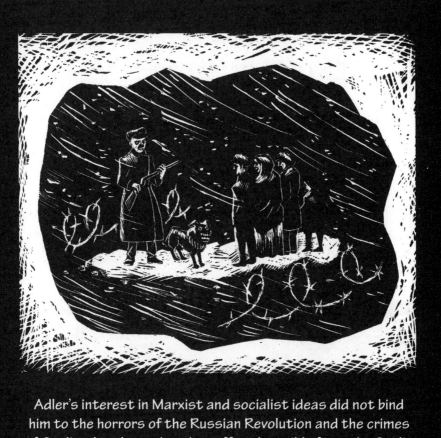

Adler's interest in Marxist and socialist ideas did not bind him to the horrors of the Russian Revolution and the crimes of Stalin. At a later date he suffered terribly from the Stalin dictatorship: his daughter Valentine was arrested and disappeared in a Soviet prison camp.

That sorrow was still to come. In 1897 Adler's life changed when somebody special appeared...

The Theory So Far

- Social interest affects our Life-style
- There is logic behind a child's attention-seeking behaviour
- Humans constantly "move" towards goals, whether or not they are aware of this
- Movement and consciousness, mind and body are inseparable

The One Big Love

Alfred Adler fell in love in 1897 and stayed that way until he died 40 years later.

It was a relationship between two powerful intellects and characters, each wanting to change the world and make a personal contribution. For long periods of the marriage the couple lived on separate continents, though during their years apart Adler returned to his country to be with his wife every summer.

Alfred Adler met **Raissa Timofeivna Epstein** in spring, 1897, probably at a political gathering. The small, fair Russian woman was already a convinced socialist with decided views about the rights of women.

Raissa was born in Moscow in November 1873. Her parents, Timofei and Anna, already had an elder daughter, Rosa. Timofei Epstein came from a rich Jewish family who owned large tracts of land near Moscow. Anna Epstein died when the girls were small and Timofei remarried, giving Raissa a half-brother. Raissa and her step-mother argued much of the time: it was not a happy childhood.

Neither was growing up socially easy. Raissa was highly intelligent and wanted to study, but Moscow University did not admit females into its hallowed halls and Russian anti-semitic feelings were strong.

Intelligent, independent and dynamic, Raissa shook the snow from off her boots and left Russia for Switzerland in 1895. She studied at the University of Zurich, taking courses in biology and zoology.

In 1897 Raissa moved to Vienna where she overwhelmed young Dr Adler with her brarins, idealism, and determination to change the world. She was different, an exotic 'new woman', with the advantage of also being a nice Jewish girl whom Leopold and Pauline would approve of.

Alfred told a friend "If I'd created Raissa in a laboratory, she could not be more to my taste!"

Alfred made quite an impression on Raissa. He was charming, attentive and idealistic. His letters were passionate and poetic. When she once broke a date he spent hours wandering the streets of Vienna and returned twice to her house to find her. Her sense of 'rebellion'

matched that of Alfred's and it must have been partly due to the excitement of their shared ideas about socialism and equality, that he fell in love. It appeared to be a perfect match.

Raissa went home in the fall with plans for a December wedding in Russia. Friends wondered if marriage was a sensible move before Adler had established himself professionally. His parents worried too. Raissa must have seemed the exact opposite of his mother, clever, assertively feminist, academic, careless of how she dressed and uninterested in domesticity. Nevertheless, the young couple were determined to go ahead.

Alfred and Raissa were married in Smolensk on 23rd December 1897. The wedding was conducted according to Jewish rites; the Adlers were not a religious family and this could be the only time Alfred took part in worship.

The newly-weds headed back to Vienna a few days after the ceremony. Alfred had been unable to rent an apartment, so his parents moved out of their place in Eisengasse until Alfred and Raissa could find a home.

Adler and Raissa were set to experience what Adler later came to term the third Life Task, that of **love/marriage/intimacy.**

Theory: LIFE TASKS

Adler believed that the human community sets three basic tasks for every individual. These are:

• **WORK**: "How to find an occupation which will enable us to survive under the limitations set by the nature of the earth."

• **FRIENDSHIP**: "How to find a position among our fellows so that we may co-operate ."

• **LOVE/MARRIAGE/INTIMACY**: "How to accommodate ourselves to the fact that we live as two sexes, and that the continuance and tolerance of mankind depends on our love life."

The early years of the marriage were happy in spite of the fact that the couple were extremely poor. In August 1898, Raissa gave birth to their first daughter, Valentine Dina. Her husband's child-rearing theories instantly began to evolve.

Their second child, Alexandra, was born 24th September 1901. Her arrival put the Adlers' marriage on the rack for a time.

The problem is a familiar one these days. But it was an unusual problem for the time. Raissa was a highly intelligent, politically aware woman of 28. She did not enjoy being stuck at home with only small children for company and chores to occupy her. Raissa wanted to be out meeting women who shared her political views and interests. She

also felt the lack of a support group. Her family were in Russia; she did not get on well with Alfred's siblings, and was not interested in becoming one of the clique of elegant, gossipy doctors' spouses.

At this stage Alfred was still a man of his time: his bourgeois consciousness needed raising. He went out and worked: his wife stayed home to care for the house and family. Alfred looked in after work briefly before heading for the Cafe Griensteidl to talk politics with other men.

When he did stay home, Adler was busy writing or studying. Raissa made him aware of this problem. Confiding in a friend, he told writer Franz Blei that Raissa was tied to the house too much of the time. He thought that when Valentine learned to walk matters would improve. (He didn't explain how). But the question of feminine equality was never in dispute with him.

Raissa was unhappy and didn't hesitate to speak her mind. In arguments, she was hard-hitting. Alfred tried to make peace. He started helping with the children and thinking more about the rights and wrongs of the way women and children were treated in general. These were his first genuine steps towards pro-feminism. Raissa was allowed more time for her career as a translator. She also enthusiastically put Alfred's ideas about child guidance into action, at times arguing fiercely with her more traditional nursemaids.

Adler's children remembered him as a caring, loving father. He never hit them; instead he explained why he wanted them to behave in a certain way. In fact the Adler's may have erred on the side of reason. Once guests were diverted by one of the children racing about the apartment armed with a carving knife and yelling: "That's made them watch me."

Theory: ADLER'S EARLY IDEAS ON CHILD REARING

Many theories, later enlarged by Adler, saw their first public outing in the Medical News Bulletin. An early paper (1904) was titled "The Physician as Educator". Adler began the paper by praising Freud, the man who'd shown how childhood experiences could cause neurotic or normal adults. He went on to postulate that the power of childhood events (coded mentally in Early Recollections) was so great that parents and teachers needed all the help they could get to let kids grow up without neuroses. And the person to help such neurotics forward should be the physicians. This is one of the earliest occasions on which such an idea had been presented.

Guidelines for positive action:

• All adults dealing with children have to gain their love. That love is the finest guarantee for educability. The child must never fear the teacher. Even when a child is naughty it must not be frightened.

• Giving children self-confidence is the best way to encourage their development. Children with confidence and courage will meet whatever fate lies ahead as something coming from within which they can alter and control.

• Pampered, over-protected and sick children have their self-esteem undermined by over-helpful adults. This has to be corrected.

• Encouragement and praise work better than threats. If you have to punish, make sure the child knows what behaviour is wrong and give them an alternative.

On October 17th, 1904 Alfred and his children, Valentine and Alexandra, were baptised as Protestants. What made Adler convert? Deep religious feeling is unlikely; he was more of an agnostic than anything else. Adler did think of God as representing a goal of perfection for humans. But Adler's most likely motivation in converting was to confirm his sense of being an ordinary Viennese citizen at a time of rising nationalism when Jews were becoming a target.

In Vienna, at that time, numbers of Jews were converting; many of them in order to get round the law banning Christian-Jewish marriages. The converts included composers Gustav Mahler and Arnold Schoenberg and Alfred's politician namesake Viktor Adler.

Whatever Adler's reason for the change, Raissa declined to convert. Nothing suggests that they ever disagreed about religion. Presumably Adler left his wife's decisions about her religious conscience up to her. Adler never developed a habit of church-going. When his son Kurt was asked if the family went to church often, he laughed: he'd entered a church only to be baptised just after his birth in 1905, and never since.

The Theory So Far

- There are three basic life tasks, work/friendship/love-intimacy

- Physicians should help neurotics forward

- Children need encouragement

The Start of a Brilliant Career

In 1898, Adler set up his own medical office at Czeringasse 7 in the none too fashionable Leopoldstadt quarter.

He also found an apartment in the same building which became the couple's first marital home. The block possessed a view over the Praterstrasse, close to the famous Prater amusement park.

Do you remember the film "The Third Man" starring Orson Welles as Harry Lime, a black market racketeer meeting an old pal and riding on the Prater's Big Ferris Wheel? Well, that same fairground provided the newly qualified Adler with many of his first patients.

The patients were mainly acrobats and clowns from the fairground and waiters from nearby cafes. The fairground people were strong and physically skilled: they needed to be in order to earn a living. It was only Dr Adler who saw their weak points and heard about their troubles. Many of the performers had started out with some kind of physical problem; they'd had to train very hard to make their bodies powerful.

Adler thought back to his own childhood, how as a sickly kid he had exercised and become a mountain climber. Like the tumblers from the Prater he had concentrated on building up weak parts of the body (in Adler's day he referred to these as "organs") until they were strong. He had positively over-compensated. Why? Because of a particular weakness: because of a sense of 'Organ Inferiority'. Here were sewn the seeds of Adler's later theories of over-compensation as the result of perceived bodily inferiority which were to prove of such seminal importance and which contributed to his split with Sigmund Freud and to the foundation of his own Individual Psychology.

A second set of patients in Adler's burgeoning practice provided him with the unlikely subject for his first book: **Health Book for the Tailoring Trade**.

Vienna's tailors and cobblers worked in squalid conditions. When Leopold Adler had threatened to make young Alfred a shoemaker he was calling up the bogeyman. These craftsmen of old Vienna were anti-Semitic but they managed to forget their prejudices when they needed the young doctor.

And they chose this particular young doctor because he was establishing the reputation of possessing a great bedside manner and an uncanny diagnostic skill, based on intuition and observation. He explained illness in non-technical language, cheered patients up with little jokes and actually listened to what they said about their health. In doing so he was completely rupturing medical tradition.

Theory: ADLERIAN COUNSELLING MEATHODS

Unlike most other schools of therapy Adlerians do not regard the counselling relationship as that between 'doctor and patient'. The Adlerian therapist has according to Rudolf Dreikurs (1967) four goals.

These are to:

1. Establish a "good relationship".
2. Find out the patient's private logic and hidden goals.
3. Help the patient understand the above.
4. Help the patient to find better goals through seeing his/her life differently today.

Such goals make it clear that the Adlerian counselling process is a co-operative learning venture on both parts, not really curing the 'sick' but teaching the unaware, guiding the lost and encouraging the discouraged. Adlerians see a counselling relationship as one between equals, where there is no superiority/inferiority issue.

Adler's book about the health of the tailors showed that the diseases they suffered from like tuberculosis, stomach pains and piles, came from their exposure to cloth dust, working hunched up and seated for hours on end in dark, airless rooms, generally the rooms they also lived in. Adler pointed out that good health goes with good social and economic conditions. Disease and depression (another problem for tailors) came out of low standards of living. Not only that, the sickness of one part of society posed a general danger to the rest.

The Health Book for the Tailoring Trade was the first printed example of Adler's specific approach to problems: in it he did more than describe bad conditions, he suggested corrective action.

His ideas included:

- **laws to set up model factories,**
- **improve housing, and**
- **fix the maximum hours a tailor should work.**

Theory: THE IMPACT OF THE OUTSIDE WORLD ON PERSONAL DEVELOPMENT

Adlerian psychology has it that we are social beings, i.e., we are born into a social group - the family - which, in turn, is part of a bigger social group, the outside world. Just as our family is of great importance in shaping our personality, therefore so too is the outside world. The way in which an Amazon Indian, for example, interprets life, believing the forest to be the world and the spaces outside the forest a dream world, clearly mean that the Indian personality will be very different from that of a Western man or woman. Certain African people have no concept of corners - these simply don't exist in their world. Their huts are rounded, tree trunks are rounded, there is nothing in the environment that contains corners. Adler's tailors, in a more immediate sense, would take their limits and their strengths from their sweatshop surroundings.

Thanks to his very personalised medical approach Adler was beginning to develop his psychiatric ideas. He told the tale of his conversation with a distant cousin. She complained of headaches, all day, every day. "So, I said to her, you can't have just a headache. Is everything all right with your marriage? That was not well received and she stamped out. But a month later she asked for a divorce."

A little later, the weekly meetings that Adler attended in Sigmund Freud's new discussion circle stimulated Adler to produce a three article series with the title "The City and The Country". In these he proved that living in the Austrian countryside was a lot less healthy than living in a town. Public health and hygiene were much better in the well-funded cities than in the villages.

As usual, Alfred put forward solutions: this time they were laws to regulate food provision and water supplies because the country shipped epidemics to the city along with such commodities.

He also penned articles urging the medical profession to involve itself with improving public health and the general welfare of the people. His sense of social interest was developing rapidly.

The Theory So Far

• **The relationship between doctor and patient (and counsellor and client) should be one of mutual respect**

• **The outside world shapes our consciousness as does the world of the family**

Adler's association with Freud was a turning point, not just in his own life but in the history of psychology.

What first connected the two men was Adler's championing of the under-dog. In 1900, before they met, Adler defended Freud's work *Interpretation of Dreams* from scornful attacks by medical colleagues. In a much later newspaper interview (1928), Adler said that as early as 1899 he attended a lecture given by Freud in order to find out what work was being done to uncover the psychological foundations of some disorders. But it wasn't till 1902 that the two great men actually met.

BIOGRAPHY

SIGMUND FREUD

SIGMUND FREUD, a Vienna Jew, was the founding father of psychoanalysis.

His great discovery was the idea of the unconscious mind. He let us see that neuroses are not so much abnormalities but rather an alternative way of functioning. Much of his psychology was based on the power and role of the sex drive. Driven out of Vienna by the Nazis, Freud escaped to England in 1938 where he continued to work and practice until his death from cancer a year later.

William Stekel, a doctor and patient of Freud's, was so impressed with the innovative way Freud had treated him, that he suggested forming a discussion group once weekly in Freud's office. The topic for discussion would be Dr Freud's new treatment approach. In the autumn of 1902 Freud invited Stekel, and two other young physicians he knew, Rudolf Reitler and Max Kahane, to join these informal talks.

On Sunday November 2nd, Freud sent an invitation to another doctor he knew only by his good reputation as a gifted diagnostician with an interest in public health, Alfred Adler.

Alfred always kept the card. Later on it came in useful to prove that Freud had approached him. The full message read:

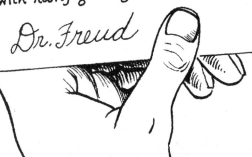

> November 2, 1902
>
> Very honoured colleague,
> A small circle of colleagues and followers is going to give me the pleasure of meeting at my house once a week in the evening at half-past eight in order to discuss the themes which interest us, psychology and neuropathology. I know of Reitler, Max Kahane and Stekel. Will you have the goodness to join us? We have agreed upon next Thursday, and I am expecting your kind answer whether you would like to come and whether this evening would suit you.
> With hearty greetings as your colleague,
>
> Dr. Freud

It was 6th November, a Thursday, when the tw men came face to face
at the first of the meetings at Berggasse 19. The subject of debate
that night was the psychology of smoking. Sigmund and Alfred both
loved to puff on large cigars.

SOMETIMES A CIGAR IS ONLY A CIGAR.

They had much in common: both trained as physicians, both were Jewish
and came from merchant families who moved to Vienna from the
backwoods. They studied at the same school (although Adler attended
14 years later than Freud) and, in the beginning, each man admired the
other. Freud considered the younger man very gifted and creative.

But they never grew close. Perhaps it was the age gap. Perhaps Adler found Sigmund Freud as bossy as his elder brother Sigmund! And there were other contrasts between the jolly, sociable Adler and the formal, messianic Freud; one was out practising medicine, the other preferred research work; Adler was a socialist and Freud, after starting out as a liberal, became conservative and snobbish.

Their wives were also very different. Martha Freud was a placid, slightly down-trodden woman devoted to housework and family life. Raissa Epstein Adler was an intellectual radical feminist with some revolutionary friends.

However the November gathering was a success. Others soon followed. Freud found himself as informal chairman of the Wednesday Psychological Society. The membership increased and included lay people, like the musicologist Max Graf.

Graf described a typical evening:

"The meetings had a definite ritual. First, somebody presented a paper. When that was over, coffee and cakes were served. Then came the discussion. Large numbers of cigars and cigarettes were smoked as we talked and talked and talked. Dr Freud wound up the discussion. He always had the last word."

Freud was pleased by Graf's attendance; he wanted to spread the word about psychoanalysis beyond the medical profession. Graf did not stay in the Wednesday Psychological Society long. He resigned, saying it felt as if a new religion was being founded.

The Wednesday group increased in size. New members had to be elected unanimously. The members (only men) were all physicians and all younger than Sigmund Freud.

Gaining Freud's Esteem

For many of these younger members there was an adventurous element to their membership into this circle where they felt like disciples.

For many of these younger members there was an adventurous element to their membership of this circle where they felt like disciples. In common with Freud, they felt criticised and persecuted by the establishment and were missionary in their zeal, fired by Freud's theories without doing much in the way of seriously questioning them. This is where Adler differed. He was not instantly or universally accepting of Freud's ideas. His critical mind made him suspicious of accepting new concepts which still needed testing. In addition, when he joined the group he was already an independent thinker on the way to important discoveries of his own and so a close bond was never established with the others. On the contrary, there were arguments. But it was Freud, at the beginning, who kept the peace.

However, Adler enjoyed the gatherings, esteemed the sharing of information and the lively debate. He respected Freud as a man who had already achieved historic progress in psychology. How much effect did Freud's theories have on Alfred's thought processes and methods of treatment? It's hard to tell. Adler appreciated the creativity of Freud's ideas and the creative atmosphere of the discussion stimulated Adler into writing and producing new theories of his own. But he was never a Freudian as such.

One theory took the concrete shape of a monograph. In 1907, Adler published his *Study of Organ Inferiority* which very quickly won professional attention. This was the only contribution of Adler's which received Freud's **unqualified** praise.

In November 1906, Adler read an important paper to the Wednesday Psychological Society, "On the Organic Bases of Neuroses" which was a forerunner to the monograph. The paper and discussion were well documented because, at Freud's suggestion, the WPS had finally hired a secretary to make detailed notes of the papers and discussions and record of the members present. His other duties included collecting subscriptions.

The secretary was **Otto Rank**, a philosophy student at Vienna University. Adler had treated the young man for a lung complaint. As doctors and patients do, they chatted about psychology. Rank attended Adler's lectures and through him was introduced to Freud. He became a regular at the Wednesday night gatherings. Otto Rank went on to become a pmajor sychoanalyst of international fame.

Theory: THE FOUNDATIONS OF THE THEORY OF THE NFERIORITY COMPLEX

Adler used his paper "On the Organic Bases of Neuroses" to give colleagues an idea of what his forthcoming book would cover. He concentrated on three ideas. These were:

1. Most neuroses grow from some form of organ inferiority that you are born with, specifically a weakness of a particular organ (body part).

2. The cause of sexual problems can be found in these same congenital weaknesses because what affects the body must affect the sex drive and the mind. This corresponded to much of Freud's view.

3. People with organ inferiority will try to compensate for their perceived inferiority so that they can fit into society. They will want to adapt and try especially hard to do so, a process Adler named 'compensation'. When people start to compensate they may not realise when to stop. They therefore over-compensate and the inferi or organ becomes superior to all the others. Adler's acrobat patients are an example of people suffering from organ inferiority.

Examples given by Adler of over-compensation were people with poor hearing who became composers, like Smetana, and public speakers who had to overcome stammers or weak voices.

Otto Rank minuted that Freud believed...

"Adler's paper has taken my work further. My first impression is that much of his paper may prove correct."

Freud contributed to the list of over-compensators the name of painter Franz von Lenbach, blind in one eye. Freud also commented that good cooks were always abnormal and his cook performed best when about to fall sick.

The Theory So Far

- People will try to compensate for their perceived inferiority

- Over-compensation leads to false superiority

Organ Inferiority

It's ironic that Freud was enthusiastic about the monograph *A Study of Organ Inferiority* since the theme of the book had extremely wide repercussions for his psychology.

But, to begin with, Freud interpreted the work as one of physiology and simply did not see its far-reaching consequences. The book was indeed influenced by Freud's concept of a 'drive' but instead of accepting Freud's notion that sexuality had the absolute preponderance, Adler instead saw a kind of democratic equality between all human drives.

ALL DRIVES ARE EQUAL BUT SOME ARE MORE EQUAL THAN OTHERS.

Theory: THE DRIVE TO FEEL EQUAL

The organ inferiority theory is at the root of Adlerian psychology. From it Adler deduced that all human beings are born with a drive to feel equal to other human beings. We come into the world as babies among a race of giants and so we start off from a position of inferiority. We unconsciously try to work away from a 'felt minus' position towards that of a 'felt plus'.

Adler further expanded the ideas already broached in the former paper on organ inferiority:

IDEA 1

Congenital organ inferiority could be minor yet become magnified by the person's subjective view of how it affects everyday living and the way in which the child may or may not fit in to the community. If the organ inferiority makes a child believe fitting in can't be done, then inferiority feelings commence and the child decides she has less value than other people.

IDEA 2

The child who feels 'organ inferior' needs careful handling. If adults criticise a child for being clumsy, weak or slow, this will over-load the already present sense of inferiority and she will grow up feeling clumsy, weak or slow. Self-worth has been scolded away. She will be reliant on others for her needs. Never encouraged, never praised, the child has low self-esteem and this becomes the pathway to neurosis.

IDEA 3

If on the other hand, the child is encouraged, she will develop the resilience and bravery to handle her sense of inferiority. This kind of child faces problems head on. She jumps at the chance to shine at the things organ inferiority could make difficult. This becomes the pathway to mental health.

Adler pointed out that 70% of art students checked had some kind of visual difficulty. Visual impairment could affect writers too. Jules Verne's sight was poor; he compensated by picturing and writing about ultra-strange worlds.

IDEA 4

The compensation process must be traversed; if an individual does not compensate, then neuroses will develop.

IDEA 5

What makes somebody over-compensate? Adler's answer was that over-compensation is a defence against the child's fear that their inferiority would be noticed by others whom they rate as superior. The over-compensator does not just attempt to be adequate but to equal the perceived superiority. She tries harder and harder. Result: over-compensation.

Adler made it clear that organ inferiority could not account for all the problems a person faced in life, nor all their neurotic dilemmas. He saw organ inferiority as one aspect of an individual's psychological character.

"The book is important for another reason, one that changed my whole thinking. You see, if compensation or over-compensation are parts of us all, they have to be the result of some basic drive. So what is the drive? Sex? No. Hunger for competence and control and acceptance in society? Yes.

"My ideas were not clear then; I needed to think more and to refine them. One thing I did know: it was not an idea to make old Sigmund happy. I let it simmer for a time."

The Theory So Far

- there may be several life forces or drives

- organ inferiority may lead to neurosis

- given encouragement sufferers from organ inferiority can overcome a tendency to neurosis

The Great Dispute

The idea of organ inferiority impressed the Wednesday night group.

Members of the group told Adler they thought the book was an important contribution to the knowledge of the physical causes of neurotic behaviour. The book also caused appreciative ripples among the Viennese medical fraternity.

Otherwise, praise was becoming a scarce commodity on Wednesdays at Freud's. (The society now included Carl Gustav Jung, another big name of the future and Sandor Ferenczi, a long time friend of Freud's and the developer of new methods to intensify the patient's symptoms in order to facilitate therapy.) The group no longer offered an atmosphere of warmth and support but instead split into opposing camps. Personal insults were hurled about. Members went in for character assassination instead of reasoned debate.

Whatever Freud may have said later, he played the peacemaker then, taking control and calming the meetings. Freud may have felt relieved that Adler was diplomatic enough not to join in the rows.

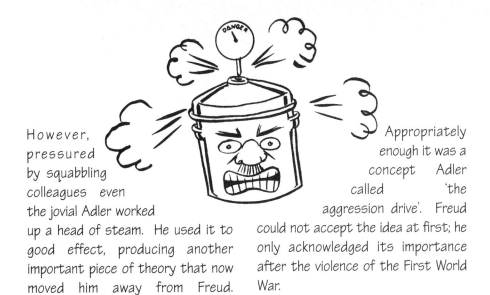

However, pressured by squabbling colleagues even the jovial Adler worked up a head of steam. He used it to good effect, producing another important piece of theory that now moved him away from Freud.

Appropriately enough it was a concept Adler called 'the aggression drive'. Freud could not accept the idea at first; he only acknowledged its importance after the violence of the First World War.

Theory: THE AGGRESSION DRIVE

In his paper 'The Aggression Drive in Life and Neuroses' Adler differentiated two drives - aggression and sex. Both were aimed at getting pleasure and satisfaction, not just in the form of physical pleasure but also through controlling the world to gratify other wishes.

"From the moment of birth, a child tries to gain pleasure. But the child is small, the world seems determined to thwart it. So a drive develops that makes the child fight for satisfaction. That is the Aggression Drive".

Aggression here means more than fighting and acting tough. Today, we would probably call it high motivation or assertion. This drive powers the whole of human consciousness and brings about good and evil.

"Attention, interests, memory, perception, fantasy, the creative drives of artists, revolutionaries and the games of children all grow from this drive. Sometimes the force turns to cruelty and warfare. But charity and sympathy and helping others also come from this power."

Violent criminal are created by the drive's dark side; the courts and legal systems come from the bright side. It can give the world Hitler and Stalin as well as Martin Luther King and Nelson Mandela.

Aggression drive is at the root of many kinds of neurotic and psychotic states. Anxiety is one common form. The drive turn inwards, seizing control of a person's system. The effects can be physical, ranging from blushing to hysterical paralysis.

Freud turned his agression drive loose in the shape of an unfavorable review. He dismissed the new theory as misleading and refused to accept the existence of any drive as powerful as that for sex.

Meanwhile psychoanalysis, although still unaccepted by the medical majority, was gaining an international reputation. In April 1910, the Psychoanalytical Convention in Nuremberg agreed to the Foundation of an International Psychoanalytical Association. Its first president—under Freud's sponsorship—was Carl Jung, while Alfred Adler became president of the Vienna organization.

The international convention was a bad-tempered affair; many of the Viennese were unhappy about Jung's selection and believed Freud had been intriguing against their interests. Freud was not averse to a little underhand plotting.

It would have seemed natural for Freud himself to take the presidency of the international organization. He declined to do so which indicated his uneasiness with the tense situation at home

Back in Vienna, Freud invited Adler to co-edit a new magazine, *Zentralblatt* (Freud, of course, would be editor-in-chief). Adler accepted and at once involved himself fully in the new analytic group.

His first job as to find a new venue for meetings. The Wednesday night group now numbered 35 and had outgrown Freud's office. Adler carried out some in-depth research into his favorite kind of conference halls — cafes!

He found a couple of promising establishments but his fellow members rejected both. Instead they hired the auditorium of the Vienna College of Physicians. The auditorium was an old, grim place with an atmosphere more like a morgue. This chilly ambience changed the Society's meetings; they became less informal, less warm and less animated.

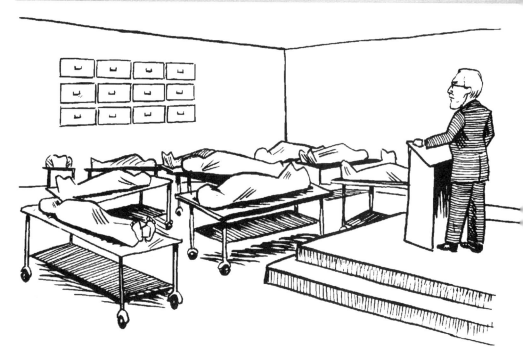

Freud was relieved that the personal insults and tantrums at meetings were now under control. He wrote to Jung saying he was pleased by the final outcome of his diplomatic handling of Adler and the rest.

His happiness was short-lived. Adler wrote an in-depth article, critical of Freud's basic theories taking him a step nearer to creating a school of psychological thought of his own.

Theory: THE INFERIORITY COMPLEX COUPLED WITH MASCULINE PROTEST

The article's title was *Psychic Hermaphroditism in Life and in the Neurosis*. For the first time, Adler presented his ideas about a subjective idea of inferiority. The great stand-by of jokers and amateur shrinks, the inferiority complex, was coming to life.

Drawing on his earlier work, Adler stated that the human drive was based on a struggle to move from a subjective idea of inferiority to an equally subjective one of superiority. The baby and the child see themselves as inferior to adults, who clearly control the world.

This sense of inferiority motivates us to seek help and explains our need to belong and fit in with t he social group. If a physical inferiority is present, or just thought to be present, a person will struggle to improve themselves (i.e. make themselves superior) through exercise. Or they will give up and grow dependent, suppressing their aggression and developing neuroses along the way.

So far this sounds much like his previous thoughts on organ inferiority but now Adler went much further. Alder named this drive the "masculine protest." In terms of our current understanding, this is a confusing name since, to us, it sounds sexist. But look at the historical context.

Adler believed in the rights and equality of women but the society in which he lived was male-dominated. Children saw a world as ruled by men. Boys naturally wanted to grow up to be strong, aggressive copies of their fathers, uncles, and big brothers. Any kind of behaviour that prevented such role-fulfillment would, Adler argued, cause a boy to protest.

*On the female side, girls and women who felt inferior were showing masculine protest when they dismiss empathy, sympathy, sensitivity and cooperation — gifts that society labels as feminine. Theirs is also a drive for power. (It's important to understand that the sense of masculine superiority is every bit as subjective as the sense of inferiority. Neither have to be **real**: you just have to think they are.)*

Adler's theory is today seen mainly as another aspect of the drive to power. Differences between male and female roles have been forcefully redefined over the past thirty years.

Adler's paper contradicted Freud's assertion of the superiority of sex drive in shaping the human personality. Freud was shaken; he saw the work of a decade belittled by Adler. He confided to Carl Jung that he thought Adler "paranoid."

A second paper of Adler's about the psychology of Marxism also upset Freud when presented to the Vienna Psychoanalytic Society.

Adler's interest in Marx was slmost certainly stimulated by two new friends Raissa brought home: **Leon and Nathalia Trotsky.**
Alfred liked Leon well enought to play chess with him and take their kids to the park at weekends.
Raissa became a dedicated long-term Trotskyite.

The Theory So Far

- Children are born with a drive to make them fight for power

- This drive has the potential for good or evil

- The 'masculine protest' is a manifestation of the drive to power where boys and girls will struggle to overcome perceived inferiorities on the grounds of gender

Dirty Words At The Crossroads:

THE SPLIT WITH FREUD

The flames of Freud's differences with Adler were certainly fanned by the group's junior members who turned the differences expressed between the two men into a struggle over Freud's personal prestige. One of them even claimed that as Freud was the discoverer of psychoanalysis it was his exclusive privilege to decide what was right and what was wrong in human psychology.

At first Freud exercised self-control and did not flare up. Gradually he showed less and less tolerance of Adler's dissent and decided his rival had to be removed from the Wednesday night group and the editorship of the *Zentralblatt*. Freud's disciple and hitman, Eduard Hitschmann, made the first move: he challenged Adler to defend his ideas to the group in Freud's presence.

Adler explained his ideas about masculine protest at two meetings. At first his ideas were attacked by Freud's followers. Secondly, Adler hit at the core of Freud's system: the Oedipus complex. ***"The Oedipus complex is just one part of psychological make-up. It's just a very powerful part of masculine protest."***

This made Freud himself speak. Bristling with hostility he proclaimed that Adler's ideas were nothing but Freud's own theories rehashed under fancy new titles. Some of Adler's theories were important, yes, but to push aside the sex drive would damage psychoanalysis.

"It (Adlerism) is not psychology: it is biology. Nothing but biology. And even if it is psychology, it's only general psychology."

"Sexual problems are part of a psychology problem but they're only covering up the inferiority and superiority struggle."

The meeting ended with Freud, cooler and calmer, admitting that Adler had offered insights but insisting his ideas were out to displace Freud's psychology of the unconscious mind with physical notions to the detriment of learning.

The society struggled on for a while with both men remaining as leading lights. Carl Furtmuller managed to force through a motion stating that the Vienna Psychoanalytical Society found the two theories **equally** acceptable. Ho, ho. Amiable Alfred Adler wanted to keep the peace. But Freud had other ideas. He waited until the summer, when many members of the group were away then wrote to Zentralblatt's publisher.

"Sir, you have a simple choice: I can no longer tolerate sharing the editorship with Herr Adler. On of us must go. You have the choice."

To his English disciple Ernest Jones, Freud ranted that Adler's new theories represented the rebellion of an abnormal, insanely ambitious person who wished to terrify others. He boasted that his letter to the publisher would push matters to a crisis.

Learning of Freud's demand, Adler voluntarily resigned as co-editor of the magazine and as a member of the Vienna Psychoanalytic Society. many of the group found Freud's manoeuvres unpleasant. Furtmuller and 11 others resigned along with Adler and wrote an open letter criticizing Freud's behavior. In his final issue of *Zentralblatt*, Adler announced his departure: Freud may have wanted him to go quietly but Adler didn't oblige. No doubt, he had no desire to appear inferior.

What really caused such an deep rift between the two men? Possibly, a fundamental reason was the contrast in their personalities. Each had a different approach to life. Freud was a man of the world, Adler on the other hand appeared as the "common man", careless of cigarette ash dropping off his sleeve.

Theory: SEX

In his own writing, Adler didn't neglect to think and write about sexuality. He didn't see sex as the primary drive in shaping personality but he certainly saw the desire for sex as a powerful component that contributes to shaping of personality formation. The bottom line is that Adlerians believe humans have a desire for sex whereas Freudians believe there is a need for it. Social opinion and cultural evaluation of sexuality plays an important role in how men and women are able to express their sexuality.

Both Adler and Freud were domineering but even here there were basic differences.

In clinical practice for example Freud made the patient lie down on a sofa while he sat behind and out of sight. Adler, on the other hand, sat his patients in easy comfortable chairs and always faced them. But it often takes one 'controller' to recognise another.

Much of their rivalry was worsened by the climate in which Freud and his followers had to contend with. Freud's theories on sexuality had attracted extreme ridicule. As a result he and his followers cut themselves off from the outside world, only inviting people to join their circle who were seen to be "one of us". When someone is as over-sensitive to criticism, as Freud must have been, it is easy to develop a kind of paranoia even when the criticism is justified.

The break however had come. Adler was now free to promote and develop his own ideas and found his own group.

Free of Big Sig's efforts to control him, Adler began to shine.

He kicked off by setting up his own discussion group: the Society for Free Psychoanalytic Study. Free because the group did not exist to promote just one set of ideas; psychoanalytical because Adler was still at work studying the causes of human behaviour and character. The group included his old friend Furtmuller, Margaret Hilferding (the first woman to have joined Freud's Wednesday discussions), the philosopher Alexander Neuer and several doctors.

And did Adler get a kick, in late 1912, out of Stekel, one of the original members of Freud's group, when he turned up at the SFPS meetings to say that Freud's discussions were now nothing but empty discussions?

The new group met in the Adler's new home. The family had moved to an up-market inner city area, at Dominikanerbastei 10, where they lived for the next quarter of a century. The apartment included an office and it was here that the SFPS gathered for discussions and coffee. Raissa Adler acted as secretary, took the minutes of the meetings and joined in the conversation vociferously.

Early in 1912 the new society started publishing its lectures as **Papers of the Society for Free Psychoanalytic Study**. These dealt not only with psychological matters but also self development, morals, philosophy and spiritual matters.

For Adler, the years after the separation from Freud became a period of rapid inner growth. Instead of having to moderate his theories continually he was able to let ideas expand. Unlike Freud, he also thrived on criticism, using it to clarify his work. And it was at this stage that he developed his warm and skillful public speaking style.

Adler never denied Freud's important influence. Both men had shown that the human personality is developed and mainly fixed during early childhood. They shared the belief that everything we do and say reveals our personalities unconsciously.

These early years of the group were a time of intense activity, inspiration and stimulation. Adler worked frantically and developed a pattern that showed up as clearly workaholic in later life. The most important early result of such enthusiasm for work and thought was the publication of his seminal text, **The Neurotic Constitution.**

In it, Adler repeated the theory that roused Frudians to howl "HERESY!"

The Neurotic Constitution

All Adler's thoughts and researches of the years came together under this title. In his book, he described how:

- The development of the individual depends on the society in which he/she lives;

- Neuroses are dependent on the psychological consequences of organ inferiority combined with secondary feelings of inferiority;

- The aggression drive is important but not as an independent force but rather as a link to all the other drives.

In his writing Adler called on literature and philosophy as well as psychology and biology to support his ideas. he quoted the **Bible**, **Homer**, **Tolstoy**, and especially **Nietzsche**.

BIOGRAPHY

NIETZSCHE

Nietzsche (1844-1900) was a German philosopher who believed that the will to power was a major influence on personal development and society.

Adler shared Nietzsche's idea that men and women who are

able to harness their internal powers for creative use were happier and more successful than those who accepted whatever cards society and life dealt them.

But Adler could not accept Nietzsche's fantasy of the Superman dominating the world.

The biggest influence on Adler's new book, however, was a philosopher, **Hans Vaihinger**, who, in 1876, set to work on a highly original study of human nature. The book wasn't published until 1911, when the author was 59.

BIOGRAPHY

HANS VAIHINGER

Hans Vaihinger was born in 1952 and started his masterpiece *The Philosophy of "As If"* when he was only 24 years old.

The central theory of his work deals with what he calls "fictions." ("Fictions" does not stand here for fantasies.)

"Fictions," the author believed, which can be conscious or unconscious, are subjective concepts by which we live. Each of us constructs a personal view of the world and when that happens to match up with something in the outside world, we accept the matching as objective truth. And truth, Vaihinger said, was only the most expedient error. It could always be different, always be modified.

Vaihinger also provided the theory of the Law of Ideational Shifts.

Theory: THE LAW OF IDEATIONAL SHIFTS

The belief is that ideas follow a regular development.

       1. Ideas start as fictions (subjective but potentially useful).
       2. They become rationalized and tested as an objective hypothesis.
       3. They are accepted as dogma.

But the process can also be reversed.

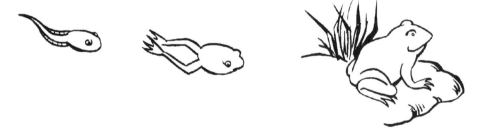

At a time when he was wide open to inspiration, Vaihinger's book provided Adler with some seminal ideas, such as the idea of acting "as if."

Theory: ACTING "AS IF"

"Acting as if..." is an action-oriented procedure used in Adlerian counselling. The idea of "acting as if" comes from Vaihinger's theory of "fictions." It is used to "move on" the sort of clients who are "stuck" and who complain "if only I could..." The counselor will suggest that, for the next week, the client should act "as if he/she can really do the things he/she wishes even though they don't believe they can." The idea has been likened to the act of wearing a different suit of clothes which sometimes gives the wearer a different type of self-image and renewed confidence.

Theory: GUIDING FICTIONS

The fictions we use to solve life's problems become our routine approaches to relationships, friends and work. Adler described them in **The Neurotic Constitution** as guiding fictions.

He believed that all the fictions we use have a purpose: to reach a **fictional final goal**. Our actions are directed towards achieving that goal, whether or not the actions appear to have that purpose outwardly or are suited to it. For example: if you want to make a hole in the wall, you can beat your head against the bricks. THe goal is fine. But the means of reaching it are not too comfortable.

One of the most important jobs Individual Psychology can do (to explain human actions) is to reveal the final goal. Adler's personal goal might have been "When my brother died, I determined to conquer death. So I became a doctor." Adler called such an aim or ambition a "fictional finalism."

The Neurotic Constitution was widely read. It spread Adler's ideas throughout Europe. He began to correspond with interested people in Russia, Germany and France. Adler's friend Furtmuller believed that the book showed how deeply and carefully constructed the foundations of Adlerian doctrines were. This was an important consideration at a time when Adler was still being passionately criticized by the friends and followers of Freud followers of Freud.

Theory: THE DEVELOPMENT OF NEUROSES

In *The Neurotic Constitution* Adler used Vaihinger's Law of Ideational Shifts to develop a concept about the process by which some neuroses might develop.

1. The fiction is a healthy person thinking, "I could get sick."
2. The hypothesis is "I am going to get sick," which shows anxiety.
3. The final dogma is the neurotic claim, "I am sick."

Increasing fame cut into Adler's free time. However, he and Raissa did manage to get Saturday nights off to drink coffee at the Café Central. They mixed with writers like Robert Musil and Franz Werfel, politicians, bohemians and oddballs like the coke-snorting anarchist Otto Gross, who also happened to be a psychologist. Trotsky was another Café Central regular. According to the head waiter, he returned to Russia, still owing for a round of coffees.

The Theory So Far

- **All humans have goals but the goals will all differ**

- **There is a distinct process that leads to neurotic development**

- **Fictions (guiding fictions) give us purpose**

The Birth of Individual Psychology

Adler's reputation grew. He addressed international meetings, wrote papers, explained and extended his ideas.

More and more, people showed interest.

At the start of 1914, Adler renamed his group the **Society for Individual Psychology (SIP)**. The new title proved the break with Freud was complete.

The group soon published the **Journal for Individual Psychology** with Furtmuller as the managing editor under Adler's benign overview.

Furtmuller's first editorial explained Individual Psychology's purpose:

"The name of Individual Psychology intends to express the conviction that psychological processes and their manifestations can be understood only from the individual context and that all psychological insight begins with the individual."

He went on to invite anyone interested to join the existing group in order to enjoy an equal exchange of ideas and support.

In America, the invitation was taken up by the leading psychologist of the day: **G. Stanley Hall**, a professor at Clark University. Hall knew Freud and had looked after him during his trip to the U.S. in 1909. Professor Hall admired Freudian theory but found Individual Psychology equally important.

Hall made his feelings public in an article that boosted Adler's compensation and overcompensation theories and attacked Freud's insistence on the primacy of sexuality. Adler and Hall exchanged enthusiastic letters; Hall started planning an American lecture tour for his new friend.

When Freud heard of this he was distressed. Recently Jung had also broken away form him, similarly finding the primacy of the sex drive hard to accept. Now Adler's growing popularity spurred him into retaliation. He wrote **The History of the Psychoanalytic Movement**, or "the bomb" as he liked to call it, which was directed specifically against the two "escapees."

The work was a blatantly biased piece of prose about the growth of psychoanalytical thought, selectively edited to leave out positive contributions made by the dissenters and deriding Adler's theories as radically false. Freud categorized Adler himself as an ambitious and messianic personality. The effect of the book was decisively to set the Freudians against the Adlerians ina serious feud that has lasted to this day. It can only be interpreted (by an Adlerian) as the work of a man who must have felt desperately threatened.

Freud's bomb was unpleasant, but it was nothing compared to the cannons that would shortly blow Europe to pieces.

A Time of Horrors: The Great War

The Great War began in late summer 1914.

The Austro-Hungarian Empire sided with Germany against England, Russia and France. Vienna bubbled with blood-lust and patriotism. Freud was excited by events and declared that his libido belonged entirely to Austro-Hungary —a statement worthy of analysis in itself! Adler's political friends, the Social Democrats, also came down in favor of conflict.

The war horrified Adler. He later said that all through the fighting he felt like a prisoner. It began badly for him since his wife and children were trapped by events in Russia. When they finally managed to return to Austria, it was in time to see Adler's magazine close after only two issues and the members of his Society conscripted. He also finally had an answer from the University Medical School to whom he had applied for a teaching post three years earlier. It was a rejection. The reason given was that his work lacked sufficient statistics. This decision was made by a neurologist known to be suspicious of all forms of psychology and psychiatry, but his word in the school was law.

Adler was crushed by this rejection but didn't have long in which to brood. Other matters rapidly occupied him. Laws on the draft were revised and he suddenly found himself back in the army and posted to a hospital in the mountains to the south of Vienna.

Army doctors in all nations shared a simple mission: to get wounded soldiers returned to the front line, the trenches, as soon as possible. The physically wounded could be healed or partly healed and sent back. But those who were shell-shocked and battle-fatigued posed a tougher problem. The official military diagnosis was always simple: "Cowardice."

Military policy therefore made hospital experience so hellish that the men were positively keen to go back to the joys of war. Doctors would use electro-shock on severely shell-shocked patients or stand them in freezing showers, then lock them naked and totally isolated in padded cells.

Adler was disgusted by such stupid inhumanity. He also felt guilty when his work demanded he return mental casualties to the fighting. he lay awake at night, horrified at the choices with which he was confronted.

His time in the military hospital produced at least one positive result however. While watching over the sleeping men, Adler perceived a correlation between the ways they lay in sleep and their behavior when awake. It confirmed his idea that movement and consciousness were inseparable and that body language made public what was always present in the mind.

Whatever his personal views, Adler the soldier worked hard. In 1917, he was moved to Cracow, a university town which was a more pleasant setting than the Austrian mountains. He sent postcards and letters home and was sad he couldn't be present when his daughter Valentine graduated. After a few months, Adler was moved to a hospital on the north side of Vienna where the patients were soldiers with typhus.

Probably triggered by the traumatic work he was forced to do, Adler reviewed some of the ideas that had formulated in his youth during the camaraderie he had so enjoyed with friends and during his early years in practice. These ideas were to do with the brotherhood of humanity. Now, spurred by the brutality of war, Adler developed his theory of social interest — "Gemeinschftsgefuhl."

Theory: GEMEINSCHAFTSGEFUHL

Adler believed the idea of social interest ("gemeinshaftsgefuhl:) might be the second great innate human drive. The first was the striving for significance ("geltungestreben"). Social interest was conceived as a counterdrive, curbing the excessive need for power.

However as the years went by, he modified the concept, seeing it no longer as an innate drive but as a potential or aptitude. He likened social interest to identification and empathy and said that social interest is "to see with the eyes of another, to hear with the ears of another, to feel with the heart of another."

It was, he thought, used to help us strive for the best goals of the community or even, in its greatest sense, for humanity as a whole. In its most positive aspect, therefore, it means co-operation and self-development of the individual's abilities for his own good and for the good of the race.

Adlerian biographer Lewis Way felt that the English translation of "gemeinshaftsgefuhl" as social interest was inexact.

"The feeling for the Gemeinschaft is wider than the term 'society' suggests," he wrote. *"It embraces the sense of relatedness, not only to the human community, but to the whole of life, and is therefore the highest expression of Adler's concept of Totality."*

It means the human being's sense of himself as part of the cosmos, or, in other words...

TRUE HOLISM.

Certainly the term "gemeinschaftsgefuhl" has many applications. It lends itself to a concept of human spirituality as in Heinz Ansbacher's short and practical explanation. "Not only an interest in others but an interest in the interests of others." Also associated with this concept is our fundamental desire to belong.

Since Adlerians have stressed the concept of social interest, counselors have learned that what the patient/client has to learn from the logic of life is not something new, but only something covered over and forgotten in the struggle to move from a "felt minus" to a "felt plus." The adlerian goal of therapy therefore is **re-education**.

Adler, during his furloughs, tested the idea among friends. The concept of equality and common interest baffled some but angered others; at least two devout followers of Nietzsche resigned from the SIP.

But regardless of how many of Adler's followers accepted his new idea, Adler himself gave increasing emphasis to his sense of the importance of social co-operation and equality at the heart of the new theory.

Theory: COOPERATION

Co-operation has become a keyword in Alderian thought. Whether or not a person co-operates may be an indication of much or how little they value themselves. Co-operation begins at birth. The "I" of the baby is confronted by the "you" of the mother. Adler regarded the child suckling at her breast as embarking on the first co-operation. The filled breast of the mother meets the child halfway.

Only the co-operation between the mother and child keeps a child alive. It is for the actual mother and for alternative "mothers" (including fathers, and close care givers) to awaken the "social interest" of the child. The task of co-operation is later extended to other carers such as teachers and other mentors.

The departure of Nietzsche's admirers may not have troubled Adler. News has seeped through from America that his books, **The Neurotic Constitution** and **A Study of Organ Inferiority**, had been translated and well received. The news boosted Adler, as did a new military post looking after wounded POWs in neutral Switzerland.

For the first time since 1915 he began to write again. In 1918, he penned half a dozen new papers, including one on war neuroses. In it he castigated low-quality military medical care and lashed the government for misusing medicine. He said the traumatized soldiers he dealt with were already neurotic and maladjusted from the civilian experiences. (Is there a smidgen of snobbery to be detected in his comment that officers hardly ever acquired war neurosis?)

His other articles were about birth order, obsessive behavior and the writer Fyodor Dostoyevski. Adler found in the works of this idealistic Russian novelist, a level of concern for others close to his own concept of social interest. This paper was presented as a lecture in Zurich, Jung's home town.

Theory: BIRTH ORDER

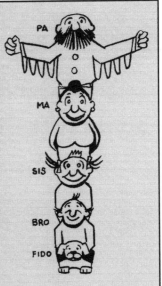

The theory of birth order has been rediscovered in the 1990s with several new books published on the subject. But Adler set out a lucid explanation of how the formation of personality may be affected by birth order well before 1920. His theory takes the common sense view that brothers and sisters affect each other and that the reason why children from the same family turn out differently is because their birth position places them under different psychological pressures which lead to differences of psychological development. Alderians have gone on to develop an understanding of traits that are usually (although not always) present in children of different birth orders.

He was still in Switzerland at the war's end. Shortly before the final cease-fire he gave a talk to the Zurich Association of Physicians where he argued that the time had come not just to cure neuroses but rather to prevent their formation in the first place. He saw Individual Psychology as a major tool for prevention. With tools like the idea of birth order and social interest, the psychology was evolving now from a therapeutic style to a major philosophic construct.

On November 11th at 11.00am, Germany and the Austro-Hungarian Empire surrendered to Britain, the USA and France. After the ceasefire, the last Austro-Hungarian Emperor abdicated. On November 12th Imperial Austria became a republic. A new order prevailed. Adler was now the citizen of a country theoretically governed by the notions of equality and fairness he had long advocated. More to the point, it was a country whose new rulers being acquaintances of the young doctor, might allow his theories to be put into practice.

Marital Change

The Adlers' marriage had endured some sticky times over the years.

Raissa had gone on to give birth to two more children, Kurt (1901) and Cornelia (1909), known to the family as Nellie. Raissa was particularly challenged by her husband's strong personality, workaholic traits and regular absences from the home.

At the beginning of the marriage the Adlers has spent a lot of time together with Adler making many friends through his wife. As we have seen these included Leon and Natalia Trotsky and Aline and Carl Furtmuller. But Raissa's passionate political views and her complete lack of interest in middle-class values meant that although she was an extremely stimulating character, she wasn't the ideal partner for a would-be upwardly mobile young physician.

When Adler's group first began meeting in the couple's home, Raissa was included both as secretary and as participant. These activities temporarily drew them together again. But this did not last long. Soon the meetings moved elsewhere and Alfred and Raissa developed separate interested separate lives. Raissa worked as a translator and political activist and found her friends amongst politicians and café revolutionaries. Alfred's theories were important and benefited humanity, she thought, but they counted for far less than political progress. By the time of the beginning of the Great War, the couple were going through a very bad patch and for the first time in 15 years separated. Raissa took the children to Russia for a long holiday.

Theory: MARRIAGE

In 1925 Adler was asked to write a chapter for a work that Jung and Havelock Ellis also contributed to: *The Book of Marriage*. In it he admitted that modern marriage was far from ideal because women were often treated as second-class beings by their husbands.. But marriage and monogamy, he felt, were still essential for society; the respect and co-operation required to make a relationship work were the highest form of social interest of which people were capable of.

In 1914, fearing that war was imminent, Alfred cabled Raissa asking her to return home at once. She characteristically cabled back: "Shall wait." Raissa had never taken kindly to being ordered about. Unfortunately, she was still waiting when the war began. As a Russian, she was now technically the enemy of her Austrian husband. But where Alfred failed to find a solution, his wife solved the problem with direct action. Somehow she

managed to see the Czar himself. She swore she was loyal to Russia and claimed she'd been forced to marry an Austrian. The Czar, out of kindness, or perhaps a wish to be left alone, allowed her to return to Vienna with her children.

They went by the scenic route — Finland, Sweden, Germany — and didn't reach Vienna until December, four months later. During this time Adler had received no news at all about them and suffered agonies of anxiety. He'd even made an abortive trip to Rome in order to try and negotiate directly with Russian diplomats. The family's return journey was an ordeal and Raissa emerged from this frightening trial strangely

altered.

A friend of Adlers, the author Phyllis Bottome, explained:

"She was no longer the ex-Russian student with all that that implied, but a balanced woman of the world, well-dressed, well-groomed, taking her place as wife and mother with dignified sophistication at first wholly strange in her. Her large and generous heart was still the same but I think it was no longer disturbed and broken. It was as if Raissa had taken a new grip on the world, and now faced it, not with the mad audacity of her youth but with a chastened and wiser courage. She had gone away wretched — like a human being who has lost her way in the world — and she came back having fought out

the battle in her own soul, like a human being who has found the way to lie, under whatever difficulties and provocations. I don't say that Raissa was any happier with Adler, for I saw no reason to suppose they were until later. But from the

time she returned from that Russian visit, Raissa was ready to play her part with strength and dignity in her own home."

Raissa had found herself torn inside by the conflicts in her marriage yet, thanks to the dangers of the war, had been forced to develop a new pragmatism. For instance, how easy can it have been for a "revolutionary" to plead with the Czar? The upshot was that Raissa continued with the marriage, for better or for worse, instead of choosing to divorce.

It was the husband of this rebellious yet newly pragmatic woman who went off to the war. And it was the war which then forced Adler to look at his own attitudes. While believing in the fellowship of men, his was the hand which sent sick soldiers back to the blood soaked hell of the trenches.

Deeply traumatic events can radically alter the confidence of previously confident and independent individuals. Both Alfred and Raissa, each in their own way, were forced to confront something about themselves due to the sufferings they witnessed. As a result, each in their own way modified their expectations. The war reinforced their belief that the pattern of family life was a priority as was the wider need to bring the means of living happily and peacefully to as many men and women as possible. In other words, their reactions to the was anchored a difficult marriage.

The Theory So Far

- Adler, for all his new thoughts on the development of the personality, believed strongly in the importance of strong family life.

New Vienna and the New Alderian Movement

The Austrian Republic, born on November 12, 1918, began life with major problems.

Poverty, hunger and galloping inflation followed in the wake of the war. The Adler family however managed well in these difficult but stirring times. Alfred and Raissa had always been careful with their money and, with some help from big brother Sigmund, and from patients who paid bills with food parecels, they survived.

The Adlers also benefitted from having friends in high places; the Social Democrats were now the dominant party in the coalition elected in 1919. Raissa had campaigned for the party and Carl Furtmuller was one of its rising stars.

Politics held no more attraction for Alfred after the war than they had before. He briefly became vice-chairman of a workers' committee, mainly because he was interested in the group's educational activities. Otherwise he stayed out of practical politics except to write a series of attacks on the communist revolution in Russia. Lenin and Trotsky's state-organised terrorism appalled him: he denounced it in articles and personally appealed to Trotsky to reign in the violence.

Rather than playing with party politics Adler involved himself in genuinely democratic work teaching psychology at the People's Institute, an adult education organisation started by colleagues like Furtmuller.

Theory: ENCOURAGEMENT

Encouragement is THE keyword in Adlerian psychology. Since we cannot change what has happened in the past, we can only change our behaviour in the here and now. If our past has made us very discouraged, change is of course more difficult.

Adlerian therapists teach their clients that although they cannot change events they can change their attitude towards these events. This can be an exciting discovery and clients are encouraged to re-write their own part in the drama in new and more self-fulfilling ways.

Parental encouragement focuses on stressing the positive and letting children learn from disappointment. It is the negative event rather than a punishment which teaches the child to change its behaviour.

Theory: TAKING RESPONSIBILITY

A typical childish cry at any age is "He made me do it". Adler took the position in these situations that we have both choice and control. Children aren't forced to go along with what their parents say. Adults don't have to continue an unhappy way of life. In short, we should all take responsibility for our lives.

It may be difficult to manage these changes of outlook. But, as assertion training teaches, if we take change slowly, step by step, we can be astonished by how much we can achieve eventually.

Teaching at the People's Institute helped Adler develop even further as a public speaker and teacher. With an audience, even a hostile one, this dumpy, middle-aged cigar-puffer became a charismatic, warm and humane speaker.

Many young people were drawn to Individual Psychology through Adler's lectures, **Rudolf Dreikurs** being one. He became Adler's leading follower and continued the development of Individual Psychology after the great man's death. He was a regular attender at the informal discussions Adler held in the "Whiff of Tobacco" café.

Another young man who came, listened and disagreed was Wilhelm Reich who later emigrated to the States and constructed a psychology based on sexual energy and his own idiosyncratic orgone therapy.

Late in 1920, Adler's first full-scale book containing all his theories appeared: *The Practice and Theory of Individual Psychology.* This brought together papers written between 1911 and 1920. Later papers dealt with post-war problems like the rising number of prostitutes and increased numbers of disturbed and criminal children.

The 1920s saw the rise of concern with issues to do with women's reproductive health throughout Europe and the United States. Contraception and abortion were hot topics. Adler joined the debate with little hesitation and controversially questioned society's right to force women to bear unwanted children. The laws remained harsh however and, perhaps concerned about associating individual Psychology with such controversy, Adler never spoke again about abortion in public.

One of the chief concerns of the new republican Vienna was school reform. It was here that the Adlerian educational ideas found a place. Troubled children had long been a concern of Adler's. He acknowledged that World War I had caused many problems but was convinced the dogmatic, authoritarian and out-dated education system had caused the child's psychological development. There ought to be, Adler felt, a university course in "curative pedagogy" — ie: teaching the best way to **prevent** or deal with juvenile crime and problems.

Theory: THE GOALS OF CHILDREN

Individual Psychology believes that people move towards goals and that these goals are unconscious ones, chosen automatically as a result of our early perceptions of life. Rudolf Dreikurs, Adler's most important follower and prime interpreter of Adlerian philosophy, reckoned that children had several such goals and he labeled what might be the four most basic ones.

1.   **Attention**. All children want attention and if they don't get it in the usual positive ways, will probably seek it negatively. Disruptive attention, even though it results in punishment, has the goal of getting bad or negative attention.   Punishment itself incidentally may still be perceived as a reward - proof at least that the child has been noticed.

2.   **Power**. All children want to feel powerful in order to prove they are valuable. So, getting one's own way becomes the goal. The child who feels positive will make positive moves for power such as studying, but the child who is discouraged may become difficult, rebellious and selfish. Punishment doesn't work in those cases since they will simply use negative methods to regain control.

3.   **Revenge**. The child who has had no success in getting parental notice resorts to getting even in order to feel it has some residual influence.

4. Inadequacy. This is a difficult goal to understand. But in appearing completely inadequate the child gains whatever scraps of attention are granted to those at the bottom of the heap. Also, if you never try, you cannot fail. So even if you don't feel you are losing much. You are enjoying a kind of psychological stasis but it's a dangerous game to play, sometimes leading to mental breakdown.

The first two goals can be used positively — the second two are always negative. And of course, although these originate in childhood, they are often deployed by adults.

As ever, Adler did something practical about teacher training besides writing articles. He became an unpaid advisor to any teacher who asked for help dealing with problem kids. A routine evolved for these sessions. One teacher would describe a case to Adler and others. When he'd asked a few questions for clarification, Adler would give an opinion on what was wrong and what remedies to try.

The method became so popular that teams of individual psychologists and teachers went from school to school in Vienna and used to interview parents and children offering advice (always with the family's consent). However, the system was criticized by some educationalists who believed children could be upset by such public questioning. Adler pointed out that private sessions were done only if asked for and, besides, the children usually enjoyed being the center of attention. Some people also felt Adler's slogan, "Anyone Can Learn," a tad over-optimistic (It was revised later on.)

The next logical step was to move from showing teachers how useful Individual Psychology was to training them in the basic theory. In 1923 a Pedagogical Institute was set up in Vienna; the following year, Adler became a professor in the Remedial Education Department as a result of popular demand by teachers. His courses included "The Problem Child" and "Problem Children in the Classroom".

Over a period of three years, 600 teachers attended Adler's lectures and learned, as Furtmuller said, "to make a reasonable guess what a child was thinking and to test the guess by the child's response to the teacher's actions."

Adler's lectures and public demonstrations of child guidance created interest in other countries. In Germany Leonhard Seif, a psychiatrist, introduced Individual Psychology courses in Munich; when Adler settled in America, Seif became the leading Individual Psychologist in Europe. Seif was the organiser of the First and Second International Congresses for Individual Psychology held in Germany in 1922 and 1925.

More interest was created when the "Journal for Individual Psychology" resumed publication in 1923 with Adler's old friend G. Stanley Hall on the editorial panel. In 1923 Adler made the first of many trips to the Netherlands and Britain. He gave a lecture at Cambridge University in German. For the rest of his life, lengthy tours of the lecture circuit became a regular feature of his routine.

The international acclaim pleased Adler but what thrilled him more was that his children Alexandra and Kurt became regulars at their fathers' meetings. Both of them became excited by the new psychological ideas of the times and both graduated to become psychiatrists in America.

Adler was rarely at home these days. Kurt and Alexandra found that the easiest way to see their dad was by attending the informal gatherings in an upstairs room at the Café Siller. Work, work and more work had become their father's routine. When he shut up the office at the end of the day, he would go to a café staying there until 2.00 am. Yet he was always up and about by 7.00 am. Somebody asked Adler how he stayed so fresh with so little sleep.

"It's very simple: I happen to be a very quick sleeper."

Trouble at the Society for Individual Psychology shifted Adler's focus from public matters to those closer to home. There were disagreements between older members and the more politically active younger members who were cranking up the tension.

The leader of the youth group was Manes Sperber, a writer the same age as Adler's son Kurt. (Kurt once said he never trusted Sperber's motives for getting involved with Individual Psychology.) Sperber went on to become a major European novelist.

Rather as Freud's group had done in the past, the Society for Individual Psychology, fragmented. It degenerated into personal insult and attack, although not to the same degree of hostility. The most serious ruction happened when a long-standing friend of Adler's, Oswald Schwarz, spoke about his new book on psychopathology to the group. Sperber and mates savaged the work for its lack of political content. Schwarz responded with a barrage of criticism aimed at Sperber and his faction. When

another senior Adlerian joined in on Schwarz's side Sperber ripped the man's notes to shreds.

The old guard expected Adler to bring Sperber to heel. But they were disappoin-

ted. All he did was to say "Maybe the boy has a point." Schwarz and several others left in silence. None of them returned. Others remained in the group afterwards but no longer felt comfortable with Adler.

Why did Adler tolerate the bad-mannered Sperber and his friends? Some people have suggested he saw his younger rebellious self in Manes Sperber; others that the young man was a substitute for

Kurt, who seemed to be drifting away from his father. Sperber offended even more people when he wrote the first biography of Adler and failed to mention most of Adler's original supporters and co-workers like Carl Furtmuller. Years later however Adler did fall out with him.

If Alfred Adler was searching for a substitute son he found a better candidate for the job in 1926 when a young Ivy League American called Walter Beran Wolfe arrived to study with him. He went on to help Alfred achieve his greatest public acclaim, in America, starting in 1926.

BIOGRAPHY

WALTER BERAN WOLFE

Born in 1900, son of a Viennese doctor living in St. Louis,

Walter Beran Wolfe attended Dartmouth College for pre-med courses. He wrote and published poems and edited a college magazine. He returned to St. Louis to study for his degree and then served in the U.S. Navy. He decided to become a psychiatrist and in 1925 became Adler's pupil.

Beran Wolfe edited and translated his teacher's works and was a major U.S. promoter of Individual Psychology. Wolfe wrote his own popular psychology books, including the best-seller *A Woman's Best Years*. He was killed in 1935 in a motor accident.

The Theory So Far

- Children and later adults work towards some specific goals These include attention, power, revenge, and inadequacy

- Encouragement helps us change our behaviour

- We must take responsibility for our behaviour

Preparing for the Pilgrimage to the New World

"The U.S.A. is like an ocean. There are infinite opportunities for people but many difficulties to overcome. Europe is a bathtub where people swim round and round with few opportunities."

—Alfred Adler

In 1926 Alfred Adler was 56 years old. During the past quarter of a century he had established a new psychology, advanced the cause of child guidance and improved teacher's education, as well as writing many books and articles. He was, by now well-known and successful. Yet he would advance to become an international speaker who attracted mass audiences and a best-selling author. Such was the impact on his life of the United States of America.

Adler planned first to visit Britain and then to continue on to the States. Aware of his limited command of the English language, he found time in his overworked schedule for English lessons. Even though his fluency had a long way to go by the time the tour departure date came around, he nevertheless decided to continue with his plans. In his view, the fact that his English was not perfect would have been the type of excuse neurotics used to explain their avoidance of real solutions to life's problems. Thus he made a point of responding to challenges.

111

Adler's theory of avoidance was often used to explain types of behavior that men and women might develop in order to help them deal with life, such as power trips. Certain behoviors seems like priorites in that they are the most likely methods to be used (unconsciously) in social situations. Control freaks, take note here!

Theory: PRIORITIES

Adlerian trainer and therapist Nira Kfir has developed this idea of priorities based on Adler's observations of avoidance. The basic idea is that life styles can be divided into four major categories:

people are either :

CONTROLLERS

COMFORT SEEKERS

SUPERIORS

PLEASERS

Kfir believes that each of these characters has developed a trait of avoidance. What they are attempting to avoid is a painful event that once paralysed them in childhood. The actual event itself has been forgotten. It is the 'scar' of the event, however, that has shaped the personality. A "pleaser" therefore, will actually be trying to avoid upsetting someone as he/she did as a child. The "pleasers" pleasing behaviour, which is to avoid rejection, is therefore, not always appropriate in adulthood - it may even displease. If you have to please at any cost, it's becomes compulsive neurotic behaviour.

Adlerian counselling sees no advantage in trying to change a person's priority. However the goal of counselling is to help the client understand the feelings that he/she arouses and the price he/she pays.

Partners are often selected as a result of their ability to let the selecting partner maintain his/her priority. Where there are marital problems, getting insight into behaviour and learning to change it where appropriate, is a counselling goal. The question to ask about a person's persistent behaviour trait is what does the client wish to avoid? The answer will always lie in the past.

PLEASE

His new American student Walter Beran Wolfe helped with Adler's English lessons. Adler eventually became a fluent, if unorthodox user of the language, retaining a strong Viennese accent, along with the Austrian habit of starting sentences with "Please". According to his friend Rowena Ansbacher, he could make "Please" mean everything from "Come in and take a seat" to "Tell me what the trouble is" or "go away" depending when and how he spoke the word.

*TRANSLATION:
COME IN AND
TAKE A SEAT.

*TRANSLATION:
TELL ME WHAT
THE TROUBLE IS.

*TRANSLATION:
GO AWAY.

Adler arrived in London in November 1936. Two groups for the study and promotion of Individual Psychology were set up. The one for doctors and psychiatrists was led by noted psychiatrist Francis Crookshank. A further group was established for people outside the medical world. The leader of this was a dynamic 40 year old philosopher with a powerful mind and a remarkable way with words: Dimitrije Mitrinovic.

Mitrinovic was responsible for a fervent publicity drive regarding Alfred Adler. However he eventually blended Individual Psychology with Nietszchean nationalism into a philosophy that became so right-wing and anti-semitic, Adler terminated the association in 1929.

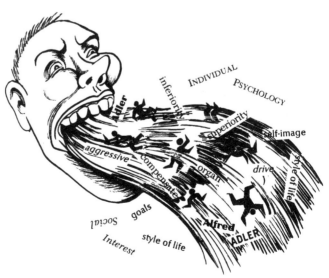

As well as setting up groups Adler lectured in London, Oxford and Cambridge. The English lessons paid off because he spoke without notes and received great applause, as he excitedly told Raissa in a letter.

At the end of November 1926 Adler sailed from Southampton on the S.S.Majestic bound for New York. The night before, he suffered a memorable nightmare - unusual for a man reported to have claimed he had stopped dreaming once he understood what dreams were for.

In his nightmare Adler was on a ship that turned turtle and sank. He survived because his willpower and determination kept him swimming until he was safe. But everything he owned went down to the bottom of the ocean.

The obvious interpretation would be nerves before an epic trip. But others have suggested the nightmare is a foretelling of the rise of the Nazis causing Adler to lose virtually everything he owned and had worked for, compelling him to re-establish himself in America.

The Theory So Far

- **Although we may appear to be moving towards particular goals, we may, in fact, be escaping past dramas. By (unconsciously) using the original mode that helped in the earlier situations, we are hoping to escape further pain, even though there is not necessarily a present threat. It is inevitable that the original mode will influence the present outcome and that the result may not always be healthy**

- **Our dreams are an expression of our Life-style and do not have universal outside meaning**

Adler Discovers the New World

Nightmares withstanding, the SS Majestic docked safely in New York.

Adler disembarked and settled into the swanky new Gramercy Park Hotel in Manhattan, beginning his American career with lectures in New York. His English was still heavily accented and sometimes incorrect but his meaning was easy to grasp. People responded to his warmth and positive manner.

The press had not covered Alfred's arrival so the public remained unaware of his presence. This changed when *New York World* ran an major interview. In it, Adler expressed his views on several topics but the one that caught public attention was his candid opinion of the Italian dictator Mussolini. The headline says it all:

NEW YORK WORLD

"MUSSOLINI SPURRED TO HIS FIGHT FOR POWER BY PIQUE OVER INFERIORITY AS A CHILD," SAYS DR. ALFRED ADLER.

Arguing that nations could suffer from inferiority as much as individuals, Adler said that the violence used by Mussolini's fascist government was a frantic attempt to give the country a feeling of superiority. The fascist movement gave the "inferior" little men of this world a chance to act tough and walk tall.

The interview included the first public expression in the United States of Adler's theory of Life Tasks.

"The behaviour pattern of persons can be studied from their relation to three things: society, occupation and sex. The feeling of inferiority affects a man's relations to these tasks. Mussolini's behaviour patterns are clear in two things - society and occupation. Of what people whisper of his "s u p e r i o r i t y complex" in sex, I have nothing to say at this time."

With a hint of mischief he added that people would be wise to worry about the p o s s i b l e failure of Italy's economy. Was he remembering that deflation doesn't just affect finances?

The headline clicked with the public. Large, enthusiastic audiences attended his January lectures. After New York, Adler began his tour in Providence, Rhode Island. He found a champion there in Sophie Lustig, born in Russia, educated at St. Petersburg University, who was married to a rich Hungarian. After meeting Adler in 1926, she became fascinated by his ideas and the man himself.

She compared the mixed gatherings of old and young, rich and poor, psychiatrists and lay people to the Greek crowds that Socrates had gathered. Adler liked to have an audience and had no snobbish feelings about who came along. The friendly American way felt congenial to Adler, in contrast to Freud, who remarked, "America is only useful to supply money."

The creator of Individual Psychology was labeled by the papers as

THE FATHER OF THE INFERIORITY COMPLEX

Others picked up on the title bestowed by an English follower:

THE CONFUCIUS OF THE WEST

119

From Rhode Island, Adler went on to lecture in Boston (including Harvard) then returned to New York and talked to members of the prestigious Child Study Association. Adler drew on his wartime observations of sleeping soldiers to illustrate how children's characters can be revealed by their sleeping postures; for example a child who pulled the sheet over his head while sleeping was far more likely to be a fearful child.

In February Adler set off on a tour of the Midwest, starting in Chicago. There he addressed a gathering of teachers so huge that over two and a half thousand disappointed people had to be turned away. From Chicago he continued to Detroit then on the Northeastern States. Wherever he journeyed he spoke to packed houses and enjoyed an excellent press.

Adler found himself fascinated by the United States, especially by the drives that he observed motivating so many of the inhabitants, economic, social and psychological. Unlike Freud, who disliked America's more modern and liberated view of women, Adler admired it. When he later returned to Vienna he talked about the central role of women in American society and of their refreshing assertiveness. But he also noted that they were paid less for work than men and lacked many privileges that men took for granted.

In April, Adler sailed for home. At this farewell there were plenty of reporters eager to record any comments the great man might let fall. They were also eager to know when he might return.

Along with the goodwill and pleased audiences, Adler left something new and innovatory behind him: the founding personnel for a US branch of Individual Psychology. Walter Beran Wolfe had the task of setting up a medical team and S.H.Hall, a professor at Columbia, was charged with establishing a branch dealing with educational psychology.

America had pleased Adler and Adler returned the compliment.
He definitely intended to return.

A year later he made the trip again. The following February (1928) he arrived for a second time in New York and this time the Press were present in strength. At a press conference, given on his arrival he stated that all psychological problems arose from troubles in the early part of childhood.

He also insisted, with some annoyance, that he was NEVER, EVER, Freud's pupil.

Adler — The Star

Adler had arrived in the States at a time when the country was ripe for him.

The advent of the motor car had given mobility and independence to young people, ideas about sex were changing radically, and the popular press was expanding rapidly. The country had a need for wise men modern enough to accept the changing situation and steady enough to impart useful guidelines for contemporary living.

It was also the beginning of a boom in best selling self-improvement books. Titles that were so far particularly successful included those on health and marriage. In the November prior to his arrival, Adler's first book of popular psychology, **Understanding Human Nature**, had hit the public. And been devoured. It was a huge best-seller. Within six months it was reprinted three times and rapidly totalled sales of over 100,000. American reviewers particularly liked its ideas on educating children towards social co-operation. Within six months, training groups and centres for parents sprang up around the country within six months and one estimate said 40,000 people took part in the parenting classes. By contrast, in the yers between 1910 and 1932, Freud's most popular book **The Interpretation of Dreams** sold only around 17,000 copies. That included UK sales as well.

Adler's February visit was in the middle of this galloping success. He explained that the book's purpose was to teach people to recognise how negative behaviour could limit their lives and to outline ways in which they might change and improve the quality of life.

Understanding Human Nature was the first of several popular books which appeared under Adler's name. They were, in fact, amongst the first 'packaged' books on psychology to be published, assembled from his notes and lectures by good editors. Beran Wolfe edited Understanding Human Nature and The Pattern of Life about child guidance. In the UK, journalist Philip Mairet assembled Problems of Neurosis and ABCs of Adlerian Philosophy from notes Adler had provided.

Adler farmed out the work because he did not really enjoy the task of writing: it used up time he preferred to expend in doing. As long as the unfinished product was accurate, he was perfectly content.

On his 1928 and 1929 tours of the US Adler taught academic courses at the New School for Social Research in New York and gave popular lectures to child guidance experts, physicians, psychologists and the public. Amongst those who heard him were the young therapists Abraham Maslow and Carl Rogers.

In 1929, Adler made friends with the millionaire **Charles Henry Davis** and treated his daughter for depression. Davis was so impressed with the results Adler got that he donated money to Columbia University to establish a teaching post for Adler. (Adler taught some fringe courses and opened a child guidance centre but was turned down for a full appointment - maybe because there were too many Freudians with tenure!) Davis later arranged a job for Adler at the Long Island College of Medicine and acted as his literary and business agent.

By the time Adler returned to Vienna for the summer of '29, he'd reached a major decision - he would re-locate in America. He resigned from his Viennese teaching and professional posts and passed the leadership of the Society for Individual Psychology to Lydia Sicher, a member of SIP since 1923.

There was only one drawback to this scheme. Raissa flatly refused to emigrate. She had her political work, her friends and family in Austria and saw no reason to uproot herself to a strange land whose language she did not speak and whose politics she disagreed with violently. The couple would spend most of the next six years apart, until the rise of the Nazi's forced her to leave Vienna in 1935.

Tales of the Vienna Woulds

Raissa had never rated her husband's work as highly as her own political strivings.

And, by now, used to her independence, little could tempt her to make such a move.

By now, she was an important figure in Austrian politics. As a long-term feminist, she may have taken pride in refusing, in middle age, to follow her husband abroad for the sake of his career. No-one knows how much the couple struggled over this separation but Alexandra and Kurt, later recalled that their parents' marital separation was amicable and indeed, every year,

Adler returned to Raissa for the summer.

For years Adler wrote to his wife regularly; that he did so, is a tribute to his continuing belief in the marital bond. For Raissa rarely replied, much to his disappointment. This lack of response came to a head in 1935, two years before his death when, depressed and ill in hospital, his plaintive letters still raised no response. A decidedly angry telegram to Raissa finally gained her attention.

And although Alfred's workaholic nature may well have contributed towards the marital drift, no doubt one of his motives for working at an exceptional pace, was to compensate for loneliness during this period. Indeed, his only method of relaxation appeared to be going to the movies. Favourite film stars,
— the Marx Brothers.

Adler's personal "stardom" may have got on Raissa's nerves too. Success in the States and in Europe must have changed him, if only to raise his confidence levels. He certainly enjoyed the material trappings of success. In America he travelled by limo.

Back in Vienna, regardless of the fact that his financial advisers told him he couldn't really afford it, he acquired a large country house - it was the lifestyle that men of success all over Europe and the United States were expected to adopt. Adler was always a man of his times.

He bought the house in 1927 but hardly ever occupied it. He would spend short visits there in summer but it was young Kurt and his bride who were the ones to move in permanently. Nor, as events proved, did he get long in which to enjoy his sense of ownership.

The Rise of the Nazis.

Adler didn't appear to notice the unpleasant atmosphere that infused the 1930 summer Individual Psychology conference in Berlin

But he did notice anti-Semitism in England when he visited in 1931. He moved to combat it. Mitrinovic, the Serb running the UK branch, had constructed a bizarre semi-mystical philosophy blending ideas from Nietzsche, Adler and others. A virulent strain of anti-Jewish fever infected Mitrinovic and some other group members.

Adler acted decisively and removed Mitrinovic. He asked the distinguished British doctor and Individual Psychologist Francis Crookshank to run the group instead. Crookshank did so for several years but then, not the best of advertisements for a psychological movement, committed suicide. Thanks to the persistence of the second (medical) group the Adlerian movement in Great Britain continued to develop. After the Second World War a new Society was formed (1952) with Dr Neil Beattie as its chairman.

In 1933 Hitler came to power in Germany, encouraging Austrian Nazis to hope they would soon be able to unite the country with Germany. Adler (applying for American citizenship) read the writing on the wall and began to fear for his family. He tried to persuade Raissa, Alexandra, Nelly and Kurt to emigrate to New York. The eldest daughter Valentine and her husband moved from Berlin to Moscow at this time.

But the family declined. Perhaps they thought Austria was immune to fascism. But it was not. Austria produced its own fascist chancellor to match Hitler: Engelbert Dollfuss. Using the suppression of a planned national strike as an excuse, Dollfuss and his para-military supporters seized power in 1934. Fighting broke out between Adler's team, the Social Democrats and the right wingers, while Raissa saw bloody action, running a First Aid post.

Dollfuss's armed supporters crushed all resistance. Some Social Democrat leaders were executed before the British ambassador convinced Dollfuss such killing was unacceptable.

A few weeks after the revolt, new laws were passed against Jews, restricting political rights and abolishing Adler's schools and child guidance centres. Carl Furtmuller was dismissed from his job, his wife was imprisoned and Raissa herself spent several nights in gaol.

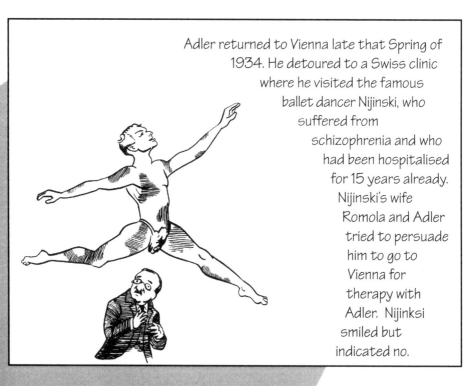

Adler returned to Vienna late that Spring of 1934. He detoured to a Swiss clinic where he visited the famous ballet dancer Nijinski, who suffered from schizophrenia and who had been hospitalised for 15 years already. Nijinski's wife Romola and Adler tried to persuade him to go to Vienna for therapy with Adler. Nijinksi smiled but indicated no.

However it's possible that just the one session Adler gave the dancer had a positive effect because for some weeks after, Nijinksy, who up till then had been completely subdued, started responding to classical music again. Nijinksi lived for a further 16 years with virtually no other improvement. Adler felt strongly that progress with such a severe illness depended a very great deal on the relationship between therapist and patient which of course he got no more chance to develop.

These were hard times for Adler. In Vienna he had to deal with the realisation that all his pioneering work of a decade had come to nothing. In addition he sold the country house, with some regrets, but at least had the satisfaction of knowing Kurt and Alexandra would move to the United States.

The combination of the worsening political situation, Alfred's abrupt decline in health and the children's emigration finally stimulated Raissa: she agreed to go to the States too but on her own terms. She would arrive in America expressly to be supportive to her husband who was recovering slowly

from illness but only provided she was able to return one more time to Vienna with him on his summer visit.

Was she brave? Or foolhardy? As a known left-winger, Raissa knew that the Austrian authorities loathed her so why did she tempt fate? Or was she choosing to live dangerously on the grounds that it gave her life added meaning?

Whatever the reason, Adler agreed and spent the summer lecturing foreign students in Vienna. Vienna was an unpleasant place to visit by then if you happened to be of Jewish blood, with many of his contemporaries dismissed from their academic teaching posts on account of their race. Adler kept a wary eye on the government but managed to avoid arrest and harassment. A personal matter caused him distress though: his assistant, friend and protégé, the young Walter Beran Wolfe died that August in a motor accident.

Knowing he was never likely to return again Adler taught two courses that summer in his old haunts at the Café Siller.

One lecture concerned the subject of what he considered to be the four human personality types.

Theory: PERSONALITY TYPES

Adler's theory of personality types is very similar to Dreikurs' eventual theory of children's mistaken goals. These personality types are:

1. **Useful**/successful at solving own problems
2. **Ruling**/dominator
3. **Avoiding**/escapers
4. **Getters**/dependents

Such descriptions were reached as a result of taking two dimensions into account.

• The first is the degree to which people manage to become socially integrated.

• The second is the manner of "movement" that individuals develop in order to integrate.

Everybody has a greater or lesser degree of "movement" towards what they perceive to be this integration.

Soon afterwards Alfred and Raissa left Austria. On the last afternoon, Adler walked his dog. The animal appeared to sense that his master was leaving. Adler assured everyone that the dog was going to a very good home but his assurances were probably aimed at himself. Especially when he anxiously voiced a fear that the new owners might not brush the animal as often as it liked.

Adler never came back to Austria.

Alfred, Raissa and Kurt landed in America in September 1935 and were greeted by a mob of reporters.

Was it Raissa's new proximity to her husband that made Alfred deliver a statement about the foolishness of thinking women to be inferior? Women's inferiority was, he announced, a male lie and repetition of the lie was responsible for women believing it.

Reunion with Raissa did not change Adler's life: he kept up a punishing schedule of lectures, clinics and interviews. He became one of the best known (and highest paid) public lecturers in the country.

To replace his gatherings at the Café Siller, Adler instituted Friday night hoe downs at the Gramercy Park Hotel. One of the Friday night regulars was young Abraham Maslow; he based much of his work on human sexuality on Adler's ideas about life tasks and social interest. Like Adler, Maslow's ideas about women were way ahead of his time; he understood that a poor self-image and low esteem inhibited sexuality. Positive self-esteem, on the other hand could increase a woman's sex drive.

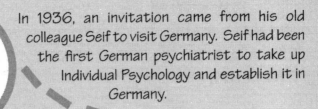

In 1936, an invitation came from his old colleague Seif to visit Germany. Seif had been the first German psychiatrist to take up Individual Psychology and establish it in Germany.

Seif swore that the Gestapo and the SS would not bother Adler. Unsurprisingly, Adler laughed hollowly and turned the invitation down.

Instead he travelled in Britain, moving from city to city, addressing teachers, the public, university students and staff and reporters, always reporters. He found time for lunch and dinner parties and therapy sessions. His secretary published a diary of a month on tour with her boss which showed he was never at rest.

In the fall he returned to New York and yet more work. One evening he announced to friends, with pride, that he had acquired a new follower: Albert Einstein.

Adler seemed to hope that Einstein would endorse Individual Psychology by declaring it the best system of psychological thought. The great relativist steered clear of favouritism however; he wrote that Individual Psychology and Freudian psychoanalysis were equally valuable.

Given Adler's final months, there's an ironic humour about an anecdote told by Sidney Roth, co-founder of the Community Child Guidance Centers of Chicago. He tells of a discussion he had with Adler about egocentricity. Adler declared that even the most egocentric person could make contributions to humanity provided he "was on the useful side of life". When might it be too late to change? asked Sidney Roth. Adler replied "Oh, maybe one or two days before he dies."

Early in 1937 Adler started planning his most ambitious European tour yet. Ten weeks in France, Holland and Belgium, then on to Great Britain for a May to July season of teaching; lectures and clinical work. The trip invluded a two week lecturing assignment at Edinburgh University. Alexandra was going to assist assist her father.

The tragic background to all this planning and feverish activity was Adler's intense anxiety about his much loved eldest child Valentine (or Vali). Vali had gone to live in Moscow with her husband in 1933 and letters addressed to her began to be returned marked Not At This Address. The same happened with telegrams. For some time the Adlers pretended the problem lay with the lousy Moscow mail service. But neither of them can have failed to consider that Stalin might be hostile towards a woman whose parents were so close to his hated opponent Trotsky.

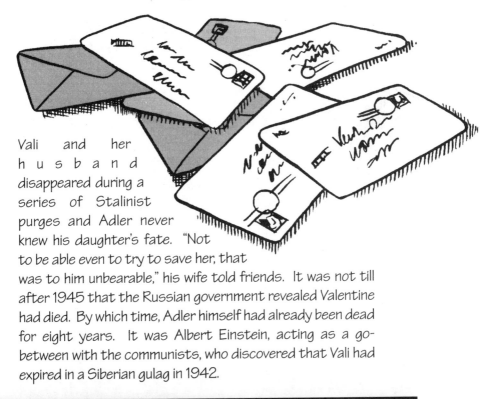

Vali and her husband disappeared during a series of Stalinist purges and Adler never knew his daughter's fate. "Not to be able even to try to save her, that was to him unbearable," his wife told friends. It was not till after 1945 that the Russian government revealed Valentine had died. By which time, Adler himself had already been dead for eight years. It was Albert Einstein, acting as a go-between with the communists, who discovered that Vali had expired in a Siberian gulag in 1942.

Not knowing where Vali was, how she was, if she were even alive, gave her father insomnia and stress symptoms. A bed chest cold made him cough blood. But the public man was unstoppable. He sailed to Europe with Raissa, settling her in Paris while he began the marathon tour in April.

In Holland Adler suffered further chest pains; medical advice was that he should take a long rest but instead, he set out for England and three days of lecturing in London.

And of course he gave press interviews. One journalist asked if Adler liked sex. The great man paused, before replying that sex was one part of the whole of a person's nature and had to be seen that way but... it was not his favourite function.

In Aberdeen, where he was booked in to speak at the university, Adler stayed at the Caledonia Hotel. Here Professor Rex Knight, organiser of the four-day speaking event, visited him. As they sat talking in the foyer, a young fellow strutted up.

"You two are supposed to be famous psychologists? Bet you can't say a thing about me."

Adler glanced at the youngster. *"Please, I can tell you this: you are very vain."*

The boy couldn't believe it. *"Why do you say that?"* he demanded.

"Because you have asked two complete strangers to say what they think of you."

On May 27th Adler wrote to Raissa about his latest plan for finding out about Vali. He intended, he said, to go to Moscow himself to ask questions. That evening he took a break at the movies with his friend Forbes-Dennis to see a film called 'The Great Barrier', about the driving of a great tunnel through the American Rockies. Adler enthused about the film, perhaps drawing parallels with his own achievements in American society.

After breakfasting on his own the next day, May 28th, Adler went for a stroll in the fresh air. A few minutes later he collapsed in Union Street.

Breathing but unconscious, Adler was taken to hospital by ambulance. But, before he got there, a massive heart attack killed him.

He was aged 67.

His wife outlived him for another 25 years, all of them spent in the country she had never wanted to settle in. She died at the age of 88. Both Kurt and Alexandra became well-known psychologists which would have pleased their father greatly and Alexandra eventually became President of both the American and the English Societies of Adlerian Psychology. Nellie, the youngest daughter, also made her home in the United States, divorcing her first husband and re-marrying in her newly adopted land.

Adler's death was reported world wide. His family and many friends attended the funeral service in Aberdeen. Tributes poured in from the many people who had worked with him or been treated by him. But there was one sour note. Freud commented that, for a Jewish boy, Adler had done very well, making a career out of contradicting … Freud.

Apart from Freud, people missed Adler. His daughter Alexandra was asked how she'd feel if her father came back to life. She replied at once. **"Enriched."**

Beyond the Grave

Some people thought Individual Psychology might not survive the demise of its creator.

They were wrong.

It foundered but then recovered. In recent years his books have been re-printed, some with new, modern translations and two international journals, in the United States and Germany, have been responsible for keeping research interest live and well.

Certain individuals have been crucial to keeping the Adlerian system, updated, extended and re-interpreted. Foremost amongst these are:

The ASNSBACHERS

Heinz and Rowena Ansbacher worked with Adler in Vienna and followed his example by moving to America. They prepared two books of selections from his work and arranged these extracts to give an overview of his thought. *The Individual Psychology of Alfred Adler* covers the earlier part of Adler's career; his later work is dealt with in *Superiority and Social Interest*.

These books, along with the work of Kurt and Alexandra Adler and Carl Furtmuller kept Individual Psychology alive in the years immediately after its founder's death. Work on developing Adlerian theory continues to this day. A major figure in the Individual Psychology movement was Rudolf Dreikurs, originally a student of Adler, who wrote one of the earliest guides to Individual Psychology in 1933.

Rudolf DREIKURS

Dreikurs followed Adler to the States in 1937 to escape the Nazis. He founded the Alfred Adler Institute in Chicago and nurtured the growth of Adlerian psychology in the States at a time when the domination of Freudian ideas made this e x t r e m e l y difficult. Dreikurs' dream was to establish child guidance centres all over the world and his understanding of children was of unique importance. His book *Children: the Challenge* is regarded as a classic work. It has also, over the years, become a best seller, notching up over 500,000 copies so far.

Dreikurs focused on children, explaining their misbehaviour by pointing out that there were goals to it. This insight was to be invaluable to parents struggling to deal with parenting problems. The fact that all behaviour has a logical motivation, even if the behaviour consists of tantrums, attention-seeking or generally "bad" behaviour , was an invaluable notion when applied to family therapy. Dreikurs believed that a client should learn something from every session.

One of his most interesting concepts was that of "the courage to be imperfect" which is also the title of his biography. The human desire to "be perfect" is at the root of many depressions and anxieties. He stressed to clients and readers that letting yourself off the hook of perfection might be the most emotionally healthy move to make.

Dreikurs was concerned with social interest and equality; much of his work was designed to teach parents how to love their children in a respectful and non-domineering manner. These ideas were vital, Dreikurs thought, if modern society was to become truly democratic for individuals and groups. His book *Social Equality: the Challenge of Today* discusses these issues in more detail.

Like his great mentor, Rudolf Dreikurs spent many of his last years travelling, demonstrating and training as many people as possible. One of his many great achievements was to devote several years intensively training an Israeli group which ultimately set up an Adlerian Institute of its own. It was work with the Israeli Civil Service Commission that enabled Dreikurs to formulate his Four Principles of Conflict Resolution, classically simple but of major importance in leadership issues.

Theory: FOUR PRINCIPLES OF CONFLICT RESOLUTION

1. **Mutual Respect.** Conflicts often arise because one or both parties are deeply discouraged, are therefore behaving negatively, thus compromising any show of respect. Managing to show some encouragement can turn a stand-off into a negotiation point.

2. **Pinpointing the Issue.** Most conflicts arise over the consequences but not over the causes of what is wrong. Getting to the real causes therefore can be crucial.

3. **Mutual Agreement.** You can't fight with someone unless you indicate you want to fight. The solution is not to force the other to change but to ask yourself "what can I do to change?"

4. **Shared Responsibility.** Decisions must be reached by a consensus, in democratic fashion. Solutions don't work if they are imposed without joint consent. This doesn't mean that everyone in a group must consent, but that a majority must.

Adlerian theory has proved so basic to the understanding of human nature that it has been used and adapted by many other psychologists.

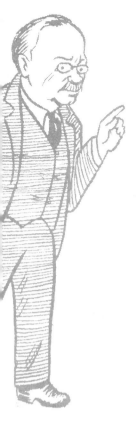

Indeed, it was so popular in the late 1920s and the 1930s that many of Adler's ideas entered into the public consciousness, lodging there in such a way that it seems as if the ideas have always existed. On one level this is gratifying to ardent Adlerians but on another, deeply frustrating. Increasing numbers of "psychologies" are emerging which their perpetrators sincerely believe to have invented. When examined however, many are shown to be using original Adlerian concepts, virtually word for word but with no acknowledgment of the debt. This ironically is why Individual Psychology has not received such a high profile as Freudian theory. It's been taken for granted. What follows is a necessarily limited list of psychologies which owe much to Adlerian psychology.

Art THERAPY

Sadie "Tee" Dreikurs, who married Rudolf, used Adlerian principles in the development of art therapy. She found that people painting, either on their own or in groups and teams, would reveal their birth order, lifestyle and main priority in what they painted and the way they set about the work.

Viktor Frankl was one of the young rebels in Adler's Viennese Society for Individual Psychology. He developed a psychology of his own, drawing on his teacher's ideas. He emerged from a concentration camp, at the end of the Second World War having learned, in the most brutal conditions, that a deep and powerful belief can help a person survive. He decided that there was a will to meaning that matched Adler's will to power and Freud's will to pleasure. Frankl called his psychology Logotherapy. Its main drive is towards helping a client face up to what has to be done in the future, rather than examine the past in order to locate the origin of a neurosis. Like Adler, Frankl leads his patients towards seeing their problems and defining the course of action needed to remove the difficulties. He also employed the Adlerian technique of paradoxical intent.

Theory: PARADOXICAL INTENT

This technique encourages clients to 'emphasise their symptoms' on the grounds that either the client will see them to be ridiculous, or will see the reality of the situation and be prepared to accept the consequences. So the woman who told Adler that she couldn't sleep a wink, was told by Adler to go to bed and deliberately try to keep awake. The woman subsequently reported that she couldn't keep her eyes open.

Cognitive THERAPY

During the last half of the 20th century there has been a rise in types of cognitive therapies, most notably Rational Emotive Therapy (RET), pioneered by Albert Ellis. Ellis believed that irrational beliefs lead to maladaptive emotional states. In therapy RET aims at making the client aware of these irrational beliefs. Aaron Beck's Cognitive Therapy is probably the most intensively-researched form of cognitive-behaviour therapy. Beck believed that depressed people distort incoming information in a negative way. This led him to teach patients to identify and modify their dysfunctional thought processes. Don't these both sound familiar?

Neuro-LINGUISTIC PROGRAMMING

The last 25 years have seen the rise of NLP, a school of psychology that pays attention to body language and to changing rigid behavioural patterns. It stresses acting "as if", sees a clear link between mind and body, recognises that childhood discouragement can affect all later life, and uses encouragement and praise, all Adlerian influences. NLP has been described as the psychology of excellence. Striving for excellence and seeking superiority are twins.

Strategic THERAPY

Strategic Therapy and Integrative Psychotherapy are amongst the most recent mutations of Adlerian thought and method. Each are psychologies of action, the first using paradoxical suggestion; the second, differing only with its seven level model of learning. Neither however pays much lip-service to its debt from Adler.

Adler would have enjoyed the parable about change. It goes: The adult children are gathered around their dying father who lies on his death bed. The son steps forward and says "Father, you are so old and wise and venerable. Tell us what you know about the future?" The old man eyes his offspring sardonically and finally whispers: "the only certainty I can give you is that nothing is certain; everything changes".

Change is what is happening now to the formation and processes of psychology. Adler, as the founder of Individual Psychology, would have appreciated this most. He put great store on "moving forward".

147

Theory: ADLER'S CONCEPT OF CHANGE

Adler firmly believed change was both possible and desirable. Men and women who become blocked in their emotions need to change. When these people's mistaken goals are revealed, they can choose to pursue them with less vigour. Adlerian counselling methods break the process of change down as follows:

1. Through therapy you can learn about your mistaken goals. Once aware of these, you can make one of two choices, either to change or not to change.

2. Through knowing your mistaken goals you begin to recognise patterns in your motivation and, as a result, develop insight.

3. Because new behaviour may work better in new situations than the old, you may be able to replace your old private logic with a new common sense.

4. As the new common sense grows you will also show more social interest. And the end result of this is that you also gain a greater sense of belonging.

5. Feeling a sense of belonging also means feeling equal to other people which also means that you are encouraged. In other words, you grow more confident of your place in the world. You feel better about everything.

6. Because you feel better about things, you become brave enough to take risks even if it means making mistakes. You have gained the courage to be imperfect.

Your new insights coupled with the new courage to act, add up to CHANGE.

THE THEORY FINALLY

Adler's theories developed and changed during his lifetime. His old friend and colleague Carl Furtmuller described the manner in which the different elements of his theory (man's striving for superiority) were first brought together in The Neurotic Constitution but then were broadened and deepened by the theory of social interest (gemeinschaftsgefuhl). As he grew older, Adler's own interest moved from focusing on the "inferiority complex" and instead strengthened the idea of social interest.

Furtmuller writes, "Now social interest became the mentally healthy direction for the innate striving towards perfection - for the individual as well as for mankind as a whole. Adler was fully aware that by this new definition social interest had left the borders of biology and entered metaphysics."

New theories based on Adler's original concepts continue to evolve with present day Adlerian practitioners working out new applications for our new times.

Adler in the 21st Century

Individual Psychology thrives.

There are training institutes in Chicago, New York and Minneapolis and hundreds of active Adlerian groups with thousands of members in Canada and the USA.

A major Adlerian movement exists in Australia and several East European countries, formerly behind the Iron Curtain, are now fighting to re-build people's every day experiences of family life using Adlerian training methods. There are active groups in Great Britain, Holland, South Africa, Puerto Rico, Ireland, Israel and Greece. After a period in the doldrums, Adler is again being enthusiastically studied in his native Austria and in Germany and Switzerland. Twenty-two countries were represented at a 1996 Adlerian International Summer School.

Adler's psychology fits a democratic era. A therapist-dominated model like that of Freud's fitted a time of autocracy when there were powerful leaders, when one man might be 'boss', when parents controlled children, even when husbands controlled wives. But we have shifted to more democratic times, when people are seen to be equal (at least in the Western world). Adler's basic approach is consistent with these times since it sees parents and children as deserving equal respect, and, where therapy is concerned, the client as a full and equal participant in the counselling process.

"No longer could man be considered as the product, pawn and victim of drives and instincts..."

Viktor Frankl's appreciation of the achievements of his former mentor focuses on Adler's "quantum leap". After centuries of people believing it is events that shape human behaviour, Adler turned this notion on its head, by stating that it is our **attitude** towards these events that counts. We are only just beginning to understand the implications of "taking responsibility for ourselves" and we have Alfred Adler to thank for it. But the very last words

should be left to the great man himself. During one of the Café Siller discussion meetings Adler told his disciples "Children, study Individual Psychology, because 50 years from now, most physicians, teachers, educators and anyone who deals with people will be unable to practise without knowledge of common sense psychiatry".

Appendix

Alfred Adler Institute of New York

30 E.60 Street
New York, NY 10022

Adler School of Professional Psychology

65 E. Wacker Place, Suite 2100
Chicago, IL 60601-7203

North American School of Adlerian Psychology (NASAP)

65 E. Wacker Place, Suite 400
Chicago, IL 60601-7203

Oregon Society of Individual Psychology (OSIP)

975 Cust Street
Eugene, OR 97405

Western Institute for Research and Training in Humanics (WIRTH)

St. Pant's Tower, 100
Oakland, CA 94610

Alfred Adler Institute of Fort Wayne

1720 Beacon Street
Fort Wayne, IN 46805-4749

San Francisco Bay Area Society for Adlerian Psychology

1580, Yalencia Street, Suit 801
San Francisco, CA 94110

CANADA

Alfred Adler Institute of Quebec
4947 Grosvenor Ave
Montreal H3W 2M2

Adlerian Psychological Association of British Columbia (APABC)
1193 Kingsway, Suit 101
Vancouver, B.C. V5V 3C9

UNITED KINGDOM

Adlerian Society (of the United Kingdom) and the Institute for Individual Psychology (ASIIP)
77 Clissold Crescent
London N16 9AR

EIRE

Irish Institute of Adlerian Counselling
2 Bromley Walk
Ardkeen Village
Dunmore Road
Waterford Eire

INTERNATIONAL

International Association of Individual Psychology
Marktstrasse 12
D-99867 Gotha
Germany
(for details of European, Asian and Australasian Adlerian Institutes and Societies)

International Committee for Adlerian Summer Schools and Institutes, (ICASSI)
Administrator
33 Leys Avenue,
Cambridge CB4 2AN
England

Recommended Reading

Adler, Alfred. (1992 new translation) *Understanding Human Nature*, (Oneworld)
Recent and very readable translation of important introduction to Adler's thoughts.

Adler, Alfred. (1992 new translation) *What Life Could Mean To You*, (Oneworld)
A popular and easy-to-read guide in a new translation. Good book to begin with.

Ansbacher, H.L. and R.R.,(eds.) (1979) *The Individual Psychology of Alfred Adler* (Harper Torchbooks)
Extracts of Adler's books, with introductory notes and comments, provides an overview of his main theories.

Dreikurs, Rudolf, Soltz, Vicki, (1964) *Children: The Challenge.* New York (Hawthorn)
A popular, practical book on how to best parent your family.

Furtmuller, C. (1979) 'Alfred Adler: A biographical essay'. *In: Superiority and Social Interest.* Ansbacher, H.R. and Ansbacher R.R. (eds). New York. (W.W.Norton)
Important source of information, especially about the break with Freud.

Hoffman, E. (1994) *The Drive for Self: Alfred Adler and the Founding of Individual Psychology.* Reading, Mass. (Addison Wesley)
The only up-to-date biography; thorough and sets Adler in the context of his time.

Manaster, Guy J. et al. (Eds) (1977) *Alfred Adler: As We Remember Him.* Chicago. (NASAP)
Family, friends, pupils and colleagues talk about Adler's life, personality and work.

Manaster, Guy, Corsini, Raymond J. (1982) *Individual Psychology: Theory and Practice.* Chicago (Adler School of Professional Psychology)
Systematic, easy-to-read explanations of all the basic Adlerian ideas and illustrates use of theories with case histories.

accept no substitute!

> Great ideas and great thinkers can be thrilling. They can also be intimidating

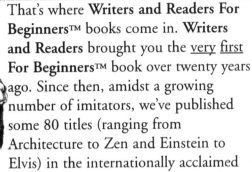

That's where **Writers and Readers For Beginners**™ books come in. **Writers and Readers** brought you the <u>very</u> <u>first</u> **For Beginners**™ book over twenty years ago. Since then, amidst a growing number of imitators, we've published some 80 titles (ranging from Architecture to Zen and Einstein to Elvis) in the internationally acclaimed **For Beginners**™ series. Every book in the series serves one purpose: to UNintimidate and UNcomplicate the works of the great thinkers. Knowledge is too important to be confined to the experts.

And Knowledge as you will discover in our **Documentary Comic Books,** is fun! Each book is painstakingly researched, humorously written and illustrated in whatever style best suits the subject at hand. That's where **Writers and Readers, For Beginners**™ books began! Remember if it doesn't say...

Writers and Readers

...it's not an original For Beginners book.

How to get original thinkers to come to your home...

Orders:

U.K

For trade and credit card orders please contact our distributor:
Littlehampton Book Services Ltd,
10-14 Eldon Way, Littlehampton,
West Sussex, BN17 7HE
Phone Orders: 01903 828800
Fax Orders: 01903 828802
E-mail Orders:
orders@lbsltd.co.uk

Individual Orders: Please fill out the coupon below and send cheque or money order to:
Writers and Readers Ltd., 35
Britannia Row, London N1 8QH
Phone: 0171 226 3377
Fax: 0171 359 4554

U.S.

Please fill out the coupon below and send cheque or money order to:
Writers and Readers Publishing,
P.O. Box 461 Village Station,
New York NY 10014
Phone: (212) 982-3158
Fax: (212) 777 4924

Catalogue:
Or contact us for a FREE
CATALOGUE of all our For
Beginners titles

Name: _ _ _ _ _ _ _ _ _ _ _ _ _ _ _ _ _

_ _

Address: _ _ _ _ _ _ _ _ _ _ _ _ _ _

_ _

City: _ _ _ _ _ _ _ _ _ _ _ _ _ _ _ _ _

_ _

Postcode _ _ _ _ _ _ _ _ _ _ _ _ _

Tel: _ _ _ _ _ _ _ _ _ _ _ _ _ _ _ _ _ _

Access/ Visa/ Mastercard/ American
Express /Switch (circle one)

A/C No: _ _ _ _ _ _ _ _ _ _ _ _ _ _ _

Expires: _ _ _ _ _ _ _ _ _ _ _ _ _ _

ADDICTION & RECOVERY (£7.99)
ADLER (£7.99)
AFRICAN HISTORY (£7.99)
ARABS & ISRAEL (£7.99)
ARCHITECTURE (£7.99)
BABIES (£7.99)
BENJAMIN (£7.99)
BIOLOGY (£7.99)
BLACK HISTORY (£7.99)
BLACK HOLOCAUST (£7.99)
BLACK PANTHERS (£7.99)
BLACK WOMEN (£7.99)
BODY (£7.99)
BRECHT (£7.99)
BUDDHA (£7.99)
CASANEDA (£7.99)
CHE (£7.99)
CHOMSKY (£7.99)
CLASSICAL MUSIC (£7.99)
COMPUTERS (£7.99)
THE HISTORY OF CINEMA (£9.99)
DERRIDA (£7.99)
DNA (£7.99)
DOMESTIC VIOLENCE (£7.99)
THE HISTORY OF EASTERN EUROPE (£7.99)
ELVIS (£7.99)
ENGLISH LANGUAGE (£7.99)
EROTICA (£7.99)
FANON (£7.99)
FOOD (£7.99)
FOUCAULT (£7.99)
FREUD (£7.99)
GESTALT (£7.99)
HEALTH CARE (£7.99)
HEIDEGGER (£7.99)
HEMINGWAY (£7.99)
ISLAM (£7.99)

HISTORY OF CLOWNS (£7.99)
I CHING (£7.99)
JAZZ (£7.99)
JEWISH HOLOCAUST (£7.99)
JUDAISM (£7.99)
JUNG (£7.99)
KIERKEGAARD (£7.99)
KRISHNAMURTI (£7.99)
LACAN (£7.99)
MALCOLM X (£7.99)
MAO (£7.99)
MARILYN (£7.99)
MARTIAL ARTS (£7.99)
MCLUHAN (£7.99)
MILES DAVIS (£7.99)
NIETZSCHE (£7.99)
OPERA (£7.99)
PAN-AFRICANISM (£7.99)
PHILOSOPHY (£7.99)
PLATO (£7.99)
POSTMODERNISM (£7.99)
STRUCTURALISM&
POSTSTRUCTURALISM (£7.99)
PSYCHIATRY (£7.99)
RAINFORESTS (£7.99)
SAI BABA (£7.99)
SARTRE (£7.99)
SAUSSURE (£7.99)
SEX (£7.99)
SHAKESPEARE (£7.99)
STANISLAVSKI (£7.99)
UNICEF (£7.99)
UNITED NATIONS (£7.99)
US CONSTITUTION (£7.99)
WORLD WAR II (£7.99)
ZEN (£7.99)

Individual Order Form (clip out or copy complete page)

Book title	Quantity	Amount
SUB TOTAL:		

U.S. only   N.Y. RESIDENTS ADD 8 1/4 SALES TAX:

Shipping & Handling ($3.00 for the first book; £.60 for each additional book):

	TOTAL	